CW01657501

Dynamic Mindset

Dynamic Mindset

Adapt Faster, Achieve More

Manuel Gonçalves

Dynamic Mindset

Manuel Gonçalves

ISBN: 978 1 7391878-5-9

Publisher: The Uplifted Publishing
Cover & Book Interior Designed by The Uplifted Publishing
Edited by The Uplifted Publishing

ACKNOWLEDGEMENT

First and foremost, I want to express my deepest gratitude to my parents, Goretti and Joao. Your love, guidance, and sacrifices have shaped me into the man I am today. The values you instilled in me are the foundation of everything I have achieved.

To my incredible wife, Marisol—thank you for always standing by me through all the ups and downs. Your unwavering support, especially during the times I wasn't there, means more to me than words can express. To my beautiful children, Jessica and Guilherme, thank you for your patience and love, even when my focus was on building the business and growing as a person. You all have been my motivation through it all.

A special thank you to my friend and publisher, Ousha Demello, for your enormous help in turning my long-held dream of writing this book into a reality. I couldn't have done it without your belief and guidance.

To my family, friends and business partners, both past and present, I extend my deepest appreciation for your belief in me and your constant support throughout my entrepreneurial journey. Your contributions have been invaluable.

I also owe a heartfelt thank you to my mentors, each of whom has played a crucial role in my personal and professional growth. Your wisdom, guidance, and memorable teachings have left a lasting impact on me, and I will carry your lessons forward:

- Matt Fiddes: "Turnover is vanity and profit is sanity."
- Alfie Best: "Don't ask a doctor to change the head gasket in your car, just like you wouldn't ask a mechanic to perform surgery. Trust the right experts for the right tasks."
- Mike Greene: "It's not where you start that matters... it's not the challenges along the way... It's where you end up that will define you!"
- Jack Canfield: "Feel the fear and do it anyway."
- Jessen James: "Step into your greatness."
- Andrew Scott: "There is always a way."
- Pet Cohen: "My intention is... now deliver it."
- Tony Robbins: "Your past does not equal your future."

Finally, to you, the reader: Thank you for picking up Dynamic Mindset and taking the time to explore these pages. I hope my experiences, lessons, and reflections inspire you to take control of your own journey, to never stop growing, and to always believe that success—both personal and professional—is within your reach.

Keep pushing forward, and remember, your mindset is your most powerful tool.

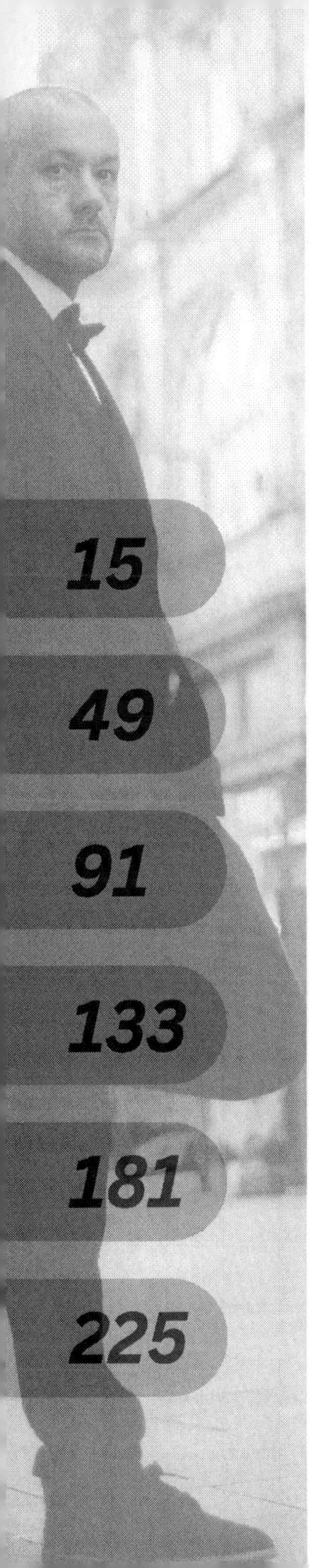

TABLE OF CONTENTS

Success is within reach;
it starts with a Dynamic mindset.

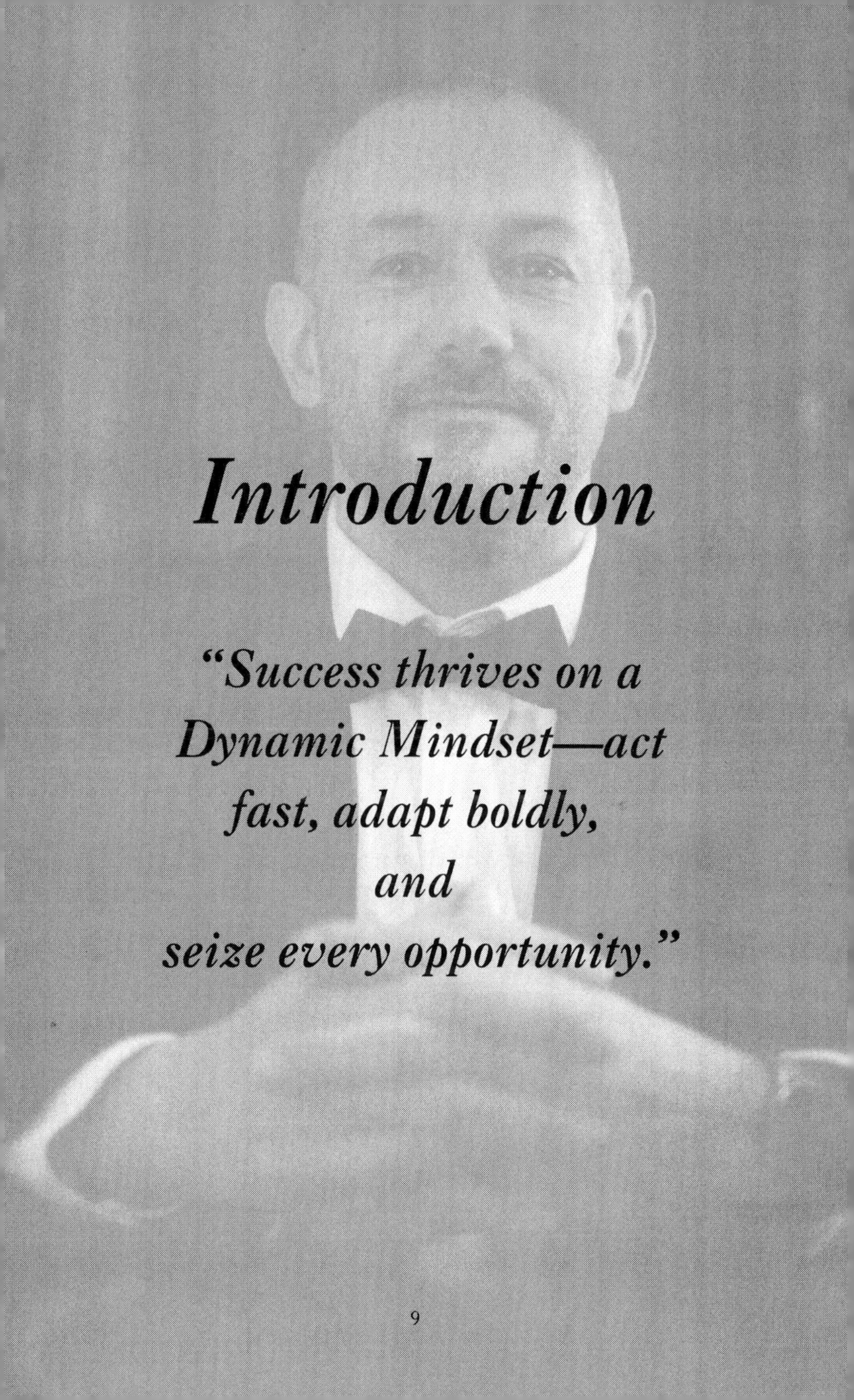

Introduction

"Success thrives on a Dynamic Mindset—act fast, adapt boldly, and seize every opportunity."

INTRODUCTION

Welcome to a journey that might change the way you look at life. In the vast landscape of life, every decision you make acts as a step along your personal and professional journey, and these steps are influenced by your internal compass—your mindset. This book explores the impact of mindset on your decisions and outlook on life, shaping it in profound ways.

Mindsets are not merely passive thoughts but powerful forces that steer our actions, attitudes, and, ultimately, the direction of our lives. They serve as the lens through which we perceive every circumstance, challenge, and opportunity. Now, picture two people confronting the same situation—say, job loss.

One person with a growth mindset might view this event as an exciting opportunity to explore new career paths, learn fresh skills, or pursue a long-held business idea. In contrast, someone with a fixed mindset might shy away from these possibilities, feeling paralyzed by fear of failure and choosing to retreat into a zone of familiarity and security.

As you can see, the difference between these two individuals lies not in their circumstances but in their reactions to them. It's not the situation that defines us; it's our mindset.

A growth mindset, made popular by psychologist Carol Dweck, emphasizes the belief that our abilities and intelligence can be developed over time.

It thrives on challenge and sees failure not as a defeat but as a stepping stone toward improvement. On the flip side, a fixed mindset is built on the belief that our abilities are static, leading to an avoidance of challenges and a preference for staying within the safety of known boundaries.

But this book takes the concept of mindset even further. I introduce to you the concept of the Dynamic Mindset—a more adaptable, action-oriented approach that thrives on the fast pace of life and positions you to seize opportunities before they slip away. The Dynamic Mindset builds on the growth mindset but goes a step further by integrating flexibility, speed, and decisiveness.

It's about more than just believing in your potential for growth; it's about training yourself to act in alignment with that belief, taking swift and bold steps when opportunities present themselves.

Consider the scenario of seeing someone you're interested in at work but hesitating to make a move. Weeks pass, and suddenly, you find out they're dating someone else—someone who took the initiative. This example illustrates the importance of quick, decisive action.

A Dynamic Mindset doesn't just recognize opportunities—it acts on them. It understands that life moves fast and life will move on without you if you don't act and adapt faster.

Having a Dynamic Mindset means realizing that opportunities are everywhere. They're not limited to significant life events; they also appear in everyday moments. Success and regret often differ in how quickly and confidently we act. With a Dynamic Mindset, you're not just hoping for growth; you're prepared to embrace it. You become the kind of person who sees opportunities and capitalizes on them swiftly and effectively.

Think about it—how many opportunities have you let pass by because of hesitation or doubt? I've been guilty of this myself. There have been moments when what I wanted most was within reach, but I failed to act. While opportunities abound, they require us to be in motion, just like the universe. A Dynamic Mindset helps you stay in sync with the pace of life, allowing you to act with confidence before it's too late.

To adopt a Dynamic Mindset is to embrace a life of intentional action. You must be clear about what you want, whether it's related to health, wealth, relationships, or happiness. The key is to remain vigilant for opportunities that align with your goals and, when they appear, act swiftly and decisively. Don't let fear or doubt hold you back.

This book is your guide to cultivating this Dynamic Mindset. It's not just about thinking differently—it's about learning to live differently. By the end of this journey, you will be equipped to navigate the rapid pace of life with clarity, courage, and a mindset that positions you to thrive, no matter what comes your way.

Let's embark on this journey together and unlock the potential within us all, helping to adapt faster and achieve more!

“*A tree with strong roots*
laughs at storms”

Malay proverb

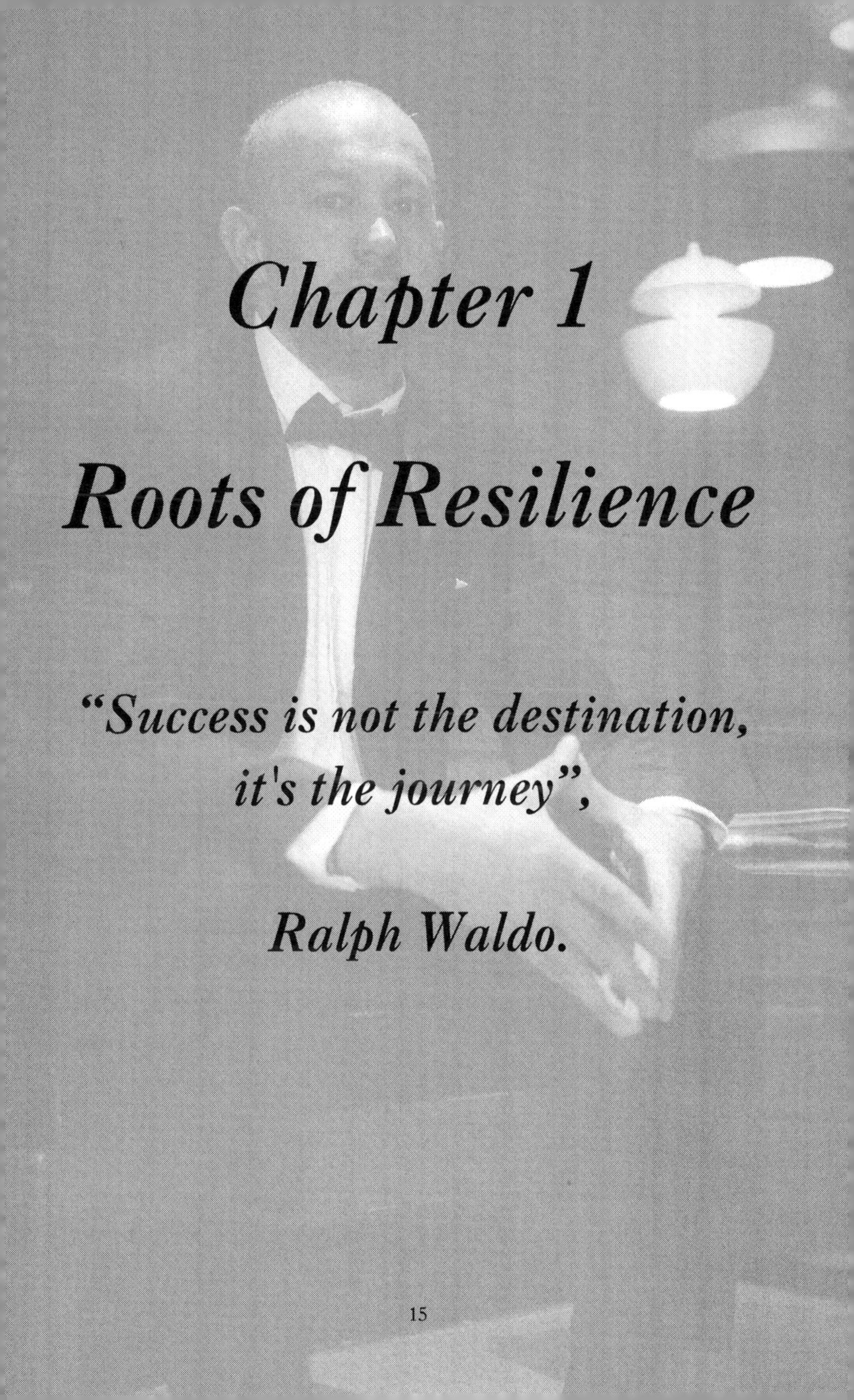

Chapter 1

Roots of Resilience

"Success is not the destination, it's the journey",

Ralph Waldo.

ROOTS OF RESILIENCE

Welcome to Chapter 1, where we dive deep into the heart of resilience. Imagine growing up in a place that felt like paradise—a childhood surrounded by nature's beauty, family traditions, and the challenges that would unknowingly shape your future.

In this chapter, we'll journey through vivid memories of innocence, hard work, and the moments that built an unshakable foundation of strength. From the joy of painting trees as a child to navigating family changes and adapting to a new life in a foreign country, these experiences reflect the roots of a dynamic mindset.

We'll explore how simple, everyday moments—like tending to a garden or watching over a magnificent bougainvillea—teach valuable lessons of dedication and adaptability. Along the way, you'll discover the importance of community, hard work, and embracing change. This chapter isn't just about reminiscing; it's about understanding how each twist and turn in life sets the stage for resilience.

Through this personal lens, you'll see that every challenge is an opportunity for growth, and every experience adds to the strength within.

So, let's walk through this childhood paradise, where the seeds of resilience were first planted, and discover how these lessons continue to bloom in life's most unexpected ways.

A CHILDHOOD PARADISE

I was born in the heart of Venezuela, at Maternidad Concepción Palacios in Caracas, surrounded by lush greenery that stretched out as far as the eye could see. Our family villa felt like a paradise—this huge, magical place that I was convinced was our own personal kingdom. It was a sanctuary, a haven of childhood magic and innocence, where the sky seemed infinite, and the land teemed with vitality. It was a childhood dreamland— Our villa stretched over 5 hectares, surrounded by an army of trees standing guard around us, the sound of birds in the morning, and endless room to explore.

Each day after school, my siblings and I embarked on joyful missions. Our delightful “duty” involved clearing fallen leaves from the ground and painting the trees up to a meter high to protect them from the animals. Though it was a chore in essence to us, it transformed into a game – an interaction with nature itself. We were not just painting trees; we were engaging in something much deeper, a bond with the world around us that taught us about dedication, responsibility, and the joy of simplicity.

Despite our tasks requiring us to paint over one thousand trees, it was a lot of fun. Our laughter harmonised with the scent of soil and the fragrant blooms that adorned the path leading to our cherished villa. With their colours and delicate petals, the flowers felt like familiar faces welcoming us each day with their enduring beauty. The connection we had with those trees was amazing and truly captured our hearts.

THE BOUGAINVILLEA: A SYMBOL OF BEAUTY AND RESILIENCE

There was this plant right by our gate, that has stayed with me in memory, a magnificent Bougainvillea plant. It was truly a sight; she was beautiful, full of leaves and those stunning pink flowers that bloomed like fireworks. The problem was we couldn't go near it because of the thorns that could easily prick you if you got too close. Despite not being able to touch it, I cherished seeing it every day on my route to school. Sometimes, my siblings and I would take a detour, walking an extra ten minutes to admire that magnificent plant. We walked along the road where orchids, roses, and other flowers lined our path. You name it! And the fragrance of all the flowers combined was out of this world. It was like walking through a paradise of nature's wonders, filling our hearts with peace and awe.

But our villa wasn't just about beauty. Let me share a bit about where the villa was located – in Ocumar del Tuy, a place that could be a bit of a dangerous area at times. Believe it or not, my dad would occasionally sleep in a tree. Isn't that something?

He claimed it was because of the heat inside the house, but we all knew he was just being extra cautious due to potential robbers in the area.

Well, you know what? We weren't the only ones staying at that villa. We had two Dobermans with us, called Brando and Violeta. Those dogs were huge and were more than just pets. They were like part of the family, there to protect us without fail. I recall this one incident when a stranger was in our gazebo, and my mum, with incredible courage, was urging him to leave. Since Dad was at work and, my brother and I, young as we were, we went to get the dogs to help her out.

When we arrived, the guy was on the side of the fence, trying to play innocent. He claimed he just needed something to eat. My mum wasn't buying his story. She recognised him from before; he had broken into our home already. The whole situation felt tense, but my mother handled it with remarkable poise. She grabs this Mossberg Maverick 5+1 shotgun—yeah, that gun—looking like she just stepped out of an action movie. It was a serious piece of hardware: five shells in the feed system, one ready to go. And she wasn't playing around. She pointed it right at the guy while my siblings and I, in full "security team" mode, escorted him off the property.

Despite the scare, we all laughed when we went back inside the house, and my mum realised that the gun was empty.

CELEBRATIONS AND COMMUNITY

Life at the villa was not all about work and vigilance but also joy and celebration. Every six months, there would be these celebrations, and when I say grand, I mean truly extravagant. We're talking about over 150 people packed into our backyard! However, my siblings and I were not allowed to participate in the festivities as children. Instead, we had to stay inside the house, but my brother and I couldn't resist peeking through the windows, watching as the adults enjoyed themselves.

On the other hand, our older sister always played it safe. She would scold and warn us that spying on the gathering wasn't proper. But can you really blame us? With so many people enjoying themselves in our own backyard, we were curious—of course, who wouldn't be?

The outdoor scene was like entering a realm. We had not one but two large gazebos, each with its substantial table. The larger gazebo could comfortably accommodate around 200 guests. For the staff members who ensured everything ran seamlessly. The other gazebo was slightly smaller but still spacious, accommodating 80 individuals. This space was reserved for executives and so forth.

Now, let me describe to you what transpired within those gazebos. There were two wood-fired brick ovens and a grand fireplace where various delectable dishes were prepared.

My mum and a team of helpers would often whip up a feast of Portuguese cuisine. The most common dish was usually "leitão" – a suckling pig between 2 to 8 weeks old. They'd place the whole pig into the brick oven, and after two hours, it would emerge a perfect light brown, ready to be the table's centrepiece. Everyone would gather around, taking pieces to their plates.

Another typical dish was "arroz de cabidela," a traditional rice dish cooked with rooster blood and bits of chicken. And my favourite was "caraotas negras," a Venezuelan dish of black beans cooked with chorizo and bits of pork. There were many other dishes, too, but let me take you to the other side of the gazebo – the barbecue area.

This was where my dad and a few others worked their magic, roasting chicken, sardines, pork, and beef. Being a barbecue lover for as long as I can remember, I always preferred this side, especially for the traditional Madeiran beef dish, "espetada." Espetada consists of square pieces of beef, skewered with bay leaves and seasoned with a mix of salt, smashed garlic, and small bay leaf pieces. Trust me, this is the best traditional food ever invented in Madeira. Next time you barbecue, try a good cut of meat like sirloin.

Back to the party – this was the food my parents used to cook for all those hungry attendees. It was a feast! A meal fit for kings and queens! The atmosphere was always lively, filled with laughter, chatter, and the mouthwatering aroma of our homemade delights.

These gatherings were more than just meals; they were celebrations of community, family, and the joy of sharing good food with loved ones. This was our culture.

Even though we were not part of the main event, we found our own ways to be involved. After everyone left, we had to pitch in with the cleanup. But first, my siblings and I had our own secret mission – treasure hunting! I always dashed straight to the smaller gazebo because I usually found coins there. Every coin I found went straight into my little piggy bank. If we found "big money" notes, we had to hand them over to Mum or Dad, but the coins were ours to keep.

One day, our treasure hunt turned to something different: a cigarette case with a few cigarettes inside. Being the curious and slightly mischievous kids we were, we decided to give smoking a try. Imagine a 5-year-old puffing on a cigarette and then nearly coughing up a lung. I thought I was going to die right there, hacking and wheezing for what felt like forever. My mum was furious when she found out. But, like with most things, the storm eventually passed, and we had a new story to laugh about after my coughing fit ended.

THE POWER OF ADAPTATION

I had a great childhood in Venezuela, filled with vibrant memories of family gatherings, delicious arepas, and playing under the warm sun. However, life had other plans for us. After years of living in our grand villa, my grandmother fell ill.

That's when my parents made a big decision—we were moving to Madeira, Portugal. It was a decision that was necessary for my grandmother's well-being. It was a significant change that required us to leave behind the world we knew and step into the unknown.

And let me tell you, preparing for that move was quite the task. We had to sell things and give stuff away—it felt like we were unloading half our lives. Little me, of course, saw this as a perfect opportunity to bring up my favourite topic: money. In my head, I still believed our villa was some kind of secret treasure trove. I figured, "Okay, we're selling stuff... so when we sell the house, we're going to be rich!" Because, in my little mind, our villa was a palace. It had this huge yard where I spent hours playing, imagining it was my own private kingdom.

One day, mid-packing, I casually asked my parents, "So, what happens to our villa now? Are we going to sell it and get a ton of money?" You know, just planning out our extravagant future in my head, as kids do.

That's when my dad hit me with the truth bomb that shattered my mini-millionaire dreams. He looked at me and said, "Uh, sweetie... it's not our villa. We were living there, taking care of it. It belongs to my boss."

Oops, I've been strutting around like a rich kid in someone else's house! I wasn't even a bit rich; I lived in borrowed luxury.

On the 31st of August 1990, we embarked on a journey that felt like the start of something new. I remember it so vividly —my grandfather, always full of quirky wisdom, loaded up the car with four big cages, each housing dozens of his trained pigeons. There were 150 of them in total, all trained to carry messages across great distances. When we arrived at the airport, he released them into the sky in this beautiful symbolic gesture of freedom and hope. It was mesmerising to watch them disappear into the clouds, knowing they'd make it back home long before we would.

In fact, they made the 30-minute flight home effortlessly, while it took us over three hours to get there by car. My grandfather often used these pigeons to send messages across town, sometimes tying a tiny piece of paper to their legs, and within half an hour, they'd be back at the loft. That day, I remember him getting a message delivered by one of his pigeons right around 11:30, as if the birds were perfectly on schedule, just like clockwork.

On the way, I remember making fun of the roads in Madeira when we first arrived. They went up, down, right, and left, twisting and turning like some kind of mad rollercoaster designed by a drunk engineer. These were not the wide, straight roads I was used to seeing in Venezuela. These were narrow and winding, and I couldn't help but laugh at how our car seemed to bounce along like it was in a cartoon. Back in those days, the trip that took us over three hours, can now be done in just 45 minutes. Progress, huh?

We finally arrived home at lunchtime on the 1st of September, and after unpacking the bags from the top of the car, we hurried inside to eat something. I was starving! Then, in the true spirit of adventure, we decided to transform the pickup truck into something more than just a vehicle—it became our mobile fortress of fun. With a surge of excitement, we installed a Capota de Carrinha com Inclinação, a slanted canopy cover over the back. Inside, we fitted long, cushioned seats along both sides, turning the bed of the pickup into a cosy lounge. It was like the ultimate hangout spot on wheels, perfect for spontaneous road trips, beach excursions, or even stargazing in the middle of nowhere. With every bump on the road, laughter echoed off the canopy, and we felt like explorers embarking on endless quests.

Three hours later, we found ourselves on the other side of the island, at a traditional party in Punta Delgada. Riding in the back of the pickup was a blast. We had fun and laughed so much on the way there and back, even though I couldn't understand a word of what anyone was saying or singing. The music was lively, and the energy was infectious. We returned home two days later, absolutely exhausted but thoroughly entertained.

Can you imagine? We had just endured an 8-hour flight from Venezuela to Porto, then a 1-hour flight from Porto to Madeira, and then topped it all off with two days of non-stop partying. We were wiped out!

It was an exhausting but thrilling introduction to our new life, and looking back, it was a move that seemed pretty good at the time. As kids, we were just thrilled to be on a new adventure.

Our arrival in Madeira marked the beginning of a new chapter. I vividly recall bringing my bicycle all the way from Venezuela. After all the excitement of arriving and unpacking the bags and boxes, I found my trusty bike. It was packed in pieces, and I eagerly started assembling it. I was in my own world for a few hours, tightening bolts and aligning wheels, determined to explore our new neighbourhood on my two wheels. Finally, with my bicycle ready, I jumped on top and prepared to ride off into the unknown. But what happened?

Just as I was about to take my first pedal, my grandmother started shouting, "Where are you going? Leave the bicycle here because you are going with us to the farm!"

My dreams of a carefree exploration were dashed in an instant. And so, my adventure took a different turn, straight into the hard work of farm life. The farm was nothing like the bustling streets and open fields I knew from Venezuela. It was a whole new world of chores, animals, and endless tasks. I had to learn quickly, and it wasn't always easy.

Life was tough for me, my brother and my younger sister. There was no room for fun or hanging out with friends after school or on weekends.

Our daily tasks involved planting crops, watering plants, harvesting potatoes, feeding the cows and everything else that needed to be taken care of on the farm.

As a child, I quickly learned that adaptability is critical to survival. You see, in Venezuela, Spanish was all I ever heard. In Madeira? You can guess! They spoke Portuguese there. I couldn't understand a word! Talk about feeling like a fish out of water. And just like that, our entire lifestyle changed, literally overnight. So, I had to learn Portuguese, adjust to a new way of life, and find my place in this unfamiliar world.

Now, let me ask you a question. Have you ever experienced frustration when trying to pick up a language?

You see, our minds are incredibly resilient. We have an innate ability to adapt, learn, and thrive, no matter the circumstances. Regardless of our origins or background, our minds have the ability to grasp and incorporate information quickly. This is a dynamic mindset: the ability to embrace change, face challenges head-on, and see every experience as an opportunity for growth.

Consider a scenario where a young child born in England suddenly moves to China at the age of five. Despite being immersed in a language and culture, the child will swiftly pick up the Chinese language and may even forget their native English. This showcases how our minds are wired to adapt to our environment, absorbing its language and customs.

I've been fortunate enough to witness this phenomenon firsthand, and guess what, not once but twice! I was born in Venezuela, South America, and I relocated to Madeira, Portugal, when I was five years old. Suddenly introduced to a language and culture, I had to let go of everything and start anew. It took me three years of effort to master Portuguese fluently and acclimate myself to my environment.

Along the way, I noticed that my grasp of Spanish and my mother tongue had faded. But life has a way of coming around. As I grew older and reconnected with friends and family from Venezuela, I found myself speaking Spanish more. It was like my mind had held onto that knowledge, waiting to bring it back when the timing was right.

So, while the journey to Madeira was filled with unexpected twists and turns, both literally and figuratively, it was an unforgettable chapter in my life. Reflecting on it now, I realise how important that experience was for developing a dynamic mindset. We were thrust into a completely new environment and had to adapt quickly. So, it's not about the situation we are in, it's how we respond to them that defines us. By embracing change and staying open to new experiences, we can develop a mindset that is not only resilient but also dynamic, always ready to evolve and grow.

As time passed, life in Madeira became more familiar, but it was not without challenges. Despite our hard work, tensions started brewing within our family.

My older sister decided to pursue a different path and moved to Funchal, a city that was three hours by bus. She was busy with her college studies and homework on weekends, so she was exempted from farm chores. Over time, her visits became less frequent as she also took up part-time jobs. She started coming home only one or two days per month. The strain in our family deepened during the one year and a half period of our parents' separation. Although I couldn't fully grasp adult relationships at that age, I could sense how it affected my dad.

Despite his challenges, he never failed to spend quality time with us. Sundays became special as we went on family trips to the beach, an escape from our day-to-day farm life.

Getting around was another hurdle we had to overcome. We didn't have a car, so we set off on a trip to Paul do Mar on foot, a charming coastal town nestled beneath towering cliffs. Walking down took 1.5 hours, while climbing up stretched to 2.5 hours. Despite the challenge, these outings became moments of connection for us.

Occasionally, we'd head out on a Saturday afternoon for a fishing adventure, camping out on the shore and returning home the next day with our catch of fish, mussels and crabs. It was a lot of fun; I remember as we walked along the path, my dad entertained us with stories from the past. He told us about the tales of struggle and strength of ancestors who trod this trail to make ends meet. They traded potatoes and vegetables for fish.

Sometimes, they go twice a day and at a very young age. A delicate balance of survival etched into our family's history.

THE BAR YEARS

Since I was young, and seeing how hard my father was working, I held onto a dream. I always say, "I'm going to retire at 42 years old". It wasn't a passing thought; it stemmed from a seated mix of fear and longing for something different. My father was often absent from our lives because he always worked hard to support our family. Seeing his sacrifices left a lasting impression on me as a child. I couldn't shake off the weight of his absence and the toll it must have taken on him.

The idea of spending my years away from my loved ones, tied to a job out of necessity, filled me with anxiety. Despite my young age, one thing I was clear on was that I didn't want to spend my life tied to work out of necessity, missing out on the joys of life and family.

In my naivety, I saw 42 as a time when one should relish one's accomplishments rather than being chained to an office or worksite. As a kid, I thought a 42-year-old man was a very old person, and seeing my dad burdened by duties and commitments that hindered his presence with his family was hard.

With Dad not being around much, I was surrounded by adults who didn't always speak the truth.

Right from the start, I realised that lies were as common as the air we breathe. However, the significant lies didn't come from others—they were the ones I convinced myself of.

Life was challenging during my childhood when I was around nine years old. When I was not at school, my days were mostly spent on the farm, working from sunrise to sunset. Even when I was at school, I had to go to the farm to do quite a lot of work after school, as it finished at 3 pm. Whether it was harvesting potatoes, tending to the cows by cutting grass for them or milking them, there was always a task at hand.

The grown-ups in my surroundings drank excessively. They would start as early as 7 am and continue until late into the night, around 10 pm, before retiring to bed and drinking all day every day again. They always offered me a glass, too.

"Just try it, "they'd say. A little wine won't hurt you. Do you want to be strong? This will make you a man and will give you power."

Initially, I believed their words held truth. What harm could one glass possibly cause? At times, the wine was mixed with frizzy drinks for the kids. The grown-ups had 1.5 L bottles of wine; for the kids, it was a 50/50 blend of wine and Laranjada. Laranjada is a frizzy drink invented in Madeira; it is sweet and has a slight taste of orange. I personally don't like it much by itself, but with wine, it tastes good.

When I was in the company of men, the alcohol would relax my inhibitions, making it easier for me to speak freely without censoring myself. And in those moments, alcohol loosened my tongue, allowing "bad words" to slip out with ease. At the time, I found it all funny, a twisted form of entertainment within the fog of drunkenness.

As time passed, when I was around 13 years old, I started going to the bar. It might not have been the spot for a teen like me, but it somehow became a familiar routine. The bar had an atmosphere where everyone appeared to be acquainted, making me feel like I belonged there despite my young age.

I always hated beer. Its bitterness didn't appeal to my taste buds, and it was pricey for someone on a budget like myself. Instead, I opted for wine. Occasionally, I'd mix it with a fizzy drink to make it more enjoyable. It wasn't the perfect combination, but it suited me just fine.

My afternoons at the bar soon became customary. I'd arrive around 4 pm and linger until around 8 pm. It was a place where I could unwind and engage in conversations with friends. We'd discuss all sorts of topics and simply enjoy each other's company through stories and laughter. Time would seem to slip until it was time to head back home.

Naturally, this lifestyle had its drawbacks, especially concerning my responsibilities as a school student.

The next day, I often found myself facing the wrath of my teachers.

"Where's your homework?" they'd ask.

I'd shrug and say, "I was working all afternoon yesterday, so I didn't have time to do it." Most of the time, it was a lie; of course, in reality, I had been at the bar.

Surprisingly, I often managed to escape without consequences. The teachers offered me another opportunity, which I pledged to improve. This bad habit impacted my academic performance, and my teacher's patience wore thin. I was gradually slipping away. I was indifferent to it all. The allure of the bar, the companionship of my friends, and the excitement of drinking were too powerful to resist. I eventually left school.

THE MONEY TRAP

When I was around 10 years old, I got my first real taste of the business world—and it all started with carrots. My mum used to give us small tasks, like helping during the carrot harvest. It wasn't just for fun either; there was a system. We'd get paid as long as we hit the target for the day. Sometimes, it was a small amount of money; other times, it was the ultimate childhood currency: ice cream. It felt like we were already wheeling and dealing, striking bargains in exchange for cold, hard cash—or cones.

But I'm going to be honest here: that early money? Yeah, a good chunk of it went to, let's say... less-than-savvy investments, like buying drinks and cigarettes. I mean, I was a kid just trying to feel a little grown-up. But that was just the start of our entrepreneurial journey. My brother, my youngest sister, and I soon found better ways to make money. We didn't know it then, but we were slowly learning the art of business.

It started when we realised the mountains near our home were full of chestnuts. On weekends, in our spare time, we'd head up there to gather as many as we could. Then, come Sunday, we'd set up shop on the side of the main road and sell them. And to our surprise, people bought them. We actually started making a decent amount of money—more than enough to take some to school and feel pretty proud of ourselves.

Seeing how well it worked, we didn't stop there. We started expanding our little "business." Potatoes, tomatoes, apples—whatever was in season and whatever our parents let us take from the garden, we turned into cash. It became almost a game for us, figuring out what we could sell next and how much we could make.

Some years later, three months before I turned 15, I completed my electrical training and secured a position as an electrician. It felt like a step into adulthood. My initial paycheck was 80,000 Escudos (€400), which seemed like a fortune for a teenager with no responsibilities and no bills to pay. My only expenses were my bike, cigarettes and drinks. By the 20th of each month, I'd usually spend all my money. I didn't mind at all. After all, at the time, for me, life was about seizing the moment, and I relished every minute of it. I worked at that company for nine months.

I've been playing football since I was six years old, sticking with it in a club until I was about fourteen. During those years, I played with and against some incredible players, including none other than Cristiano Ronaldo. As you might guess, I wasn't quite at his level, but I could hold my own on the field. When I stopped playing for the team, I didn't give up football altogether. Instead, I started playing casually with friends every Sunday.

One Sunday afternoon, while playing football, as usual, a man approached me. He introduced himself and offered me a job at his company with a salary of 115,000 Escudos (€550). It was quite the raise. Without hesitation, I accepted his offer. Although I told him I needed to provide notice to my employer for a week before joining his team, I already envisioned how much extra money this new opportunity would bring.

The initial months at the workplace were fantastic. With an increased salary, I believed I'd finally have enough to last the whole month. But it didn't take long for reality to set in. By the 15th of each month, I found myself broke again. It just didn't add up. How was it possible that despite making more money, I was running out of money faster?

Why were my friends, who earned less than me, able to afford more outings and drinks? It puzzled me. They seemed to handle their finances, leaving me questioning where I had gone wrong.

One day, I confided in an older friend about my woes. I expressed my frustration about how my money seemed to disappear even though my earnings had increased. He listened attentively and shared a piece of advice that stuck with me: "It is not the money you earn but the money you spend."

His words resonated with me at that moment. However, I still struggled to grasp the idea. Looking back, I now see that my spending habits were really getting out of hand. The excitement of making money led me to splurge. Going out for nights at the bar, indulging in luxuries, and not keeping tabs on my expenses all added up quickly. My friend gave me the right advice.

My friend gave me the right advice, but I was too caught up in the thrill of having more cash to truly take it to heart. I remember vividly in December 2000, we worked every day from the 1st to the 20th, from 8 am to 2 am, trying to finish a hotel project. On the 21st of December, I got paid 293,000 Escudos (€1465), and then the company closed for holidays until January. On the 1st of January, 2001, we switched to the euro. I remember going to the cash point on the 3rd of January and seeing only €36 left in my account.

Despite working so hard and nearly tripling my salary, I hadn't managed enough money to make it last even a month. With the next payday a month away on the 1st of February, I realised I had to learn how to manage my money better.

This experience was a harsh lesson in financial responsibility. Working hard and earning more isn't enough if you don't know how to manage your finances wisely. It was a wake-up call that I desperately needed.

Those were the years when I faced a reality: just because you earn more doesn't mean you end up with more. It took time for this lesson to sink in, but it became one of the most valuable lessons I've ever learned. The issue wasn't my income; it was my mindset. Without changing my mindset first, no sum of money would ever feel sufficient.

As the years passed, I noticed myself maturing quicker than I ever expected. The money I earned gave me a sense of freedom and independence, and I decided to try out new things and started enjoying Jack Daniels. Beer just wasn't my cup of tea. While my friends stuck to their brews, I proudly sipped my JD and Coke. In my mind, this made me the cool one. After all, I was drinking the stronger, more expensive stuff.

We spent much of our time at the local bar, which had become our hangout spot. But it wasn't just about the drinking; we were also there for the girls.

They would come in for a juice or an ice cream. We'd watch them while trying to impress them with our confidence and style. Holding onto my Jack Daniels glass made me feel like a standout, believing it added a touch of maturity and sophistication. Consequently, my drinking habit intensified —mornings filled with headaches that made it seem like my head was about to split.

Between 15 and 17 years old, drinking alcohol was no longer about fitting in; it became a regular part of my life. On days of the week, you'd often see me holding a drink in my hand. Occasionally, I indulged in a whole bottle of Jack Daniels by myself. The sensation of the whiskey trickling down my throat, followed by that buzz – became a craving for me.

However, along with the drinking came a darker side. There were evenings when I would wake up without any recollection of how I made it back home. One day, three friends and I planned to go to a party in the next village. We started drinking in our village, and by the time we arrived, we still had a ten-minute walk ahead of us. So, what did we do? We decided to buy two JD bottles and finished one quite quickly. As the night went on, our excitement turned into chaos. We were stumbling around, laughing loudly, and generally making fools of ourselves.

Long story short, we were so drunk by the time we reached the party that they wouldn't let us in. Dejected and even more unsteady on our feet, we began the 45-minute trek back home—a walk I don't remember at all.

When I finally got home, I accidentally stumbled into my parents' bed. Thinking it was my brother in my bed, I started shouting. My dad spoke, a voice cut through my confusion, and in that instant, my drunkenness seemed to vanish.

Those years were a blur of alcohol, fleeting moments of joy, and an undercurrent of something darker that I couldn't quite name. It was a time of pretending to be something I wasn't and escaping from realities I wasn't ready to face. And though I thought I was the cool one, in truth, I was just a kid lost in the chaos of growing up too fast.

PLANTING THE SEEDS OF SUCCESS

Now, I am sure that after what I am about to share with you, you will never look at a tree the same way again. Intrigued? Well, "A tree has to grow in two directions". Imagine how a tree stands tall, its branches reaching for the sky and its roots firmly grounded in the earth below. This beautiful sight conveys a message about the essence of progress and accomplishment. Like how a tree grows upwards towards the sun and downwards into the ground, our personal growth also involves expanding in directions. You see, the roots represent our journey of growth and development, which begins within our minds – the core foundation of our existence.

Our brains serve as a network of roots, akin to those of a tree spreading out and establishing connections based on our interactions and beliefs.

Similar to how a tree's roots support its growth, if the neurocognition in our brain does not align with our goals, then realising them would become challenging.

What's intriguing is that our brains possess potential; they blur the line between what's real and what is imagined. That means that by affirming our goals in the present tense, we can actually start to plant the seeds of success in our minds. You see, from birth, we possess the ability to mould our mindset. However, as we mature, external influences shape us.

Occasionally, these influences are beneficial, and often, they're not so favourable. During the years from 0 to 7, we absorb information like sponges from our surroundings. We aim to construct the best mindset but frequently end up conditioned by our caregivers—parents or teachers—and other adult figures in our lives. It is like they are crafting the blueprint for our thoughts without us being aware of it.

Consequently, as we absorb life's lessons, we often discover that they come with baggage. This baggage consists of the messages we receive from those around us, statements like "You can't do that" or "That's impossible."

Similar to a computer infected with software, these messages can distort our thinking and hinder our growth. As we mature, these messages become ingrained in our minds, leading us to believe that certain things are beyond our reach.

That's why it is essential to clear out the mental clutter and redefine ourselves for success.

Bruce Lee's enduring wisdom strikes a chord when it comes to resetting our programming. He famously advised the following: "Empty your mind. Be formless, shapeless like water. Now, you put water into a cup; it becomes the cup. You put water into a bottle; it becomes the bottle. You put water in a teapot; it becomes the teapot. Now water can flow, or it can crash. Be water, my friend."

What does this truly entail?

To authentically alter our programming, we must first free our minds of beliefs that constrain us. These beliefs are also called limiting beliefs. Just as a cup must be emptied before it can be refilled, we need to discard the programs that no longer serve us well. We make room for ideas and opportunities to flourish when we release these barriers.

We need to embrace adaptability and openness in our thoughts. Holding onto beliefs and fixed notions can hinder our ability to evolve and adjust. Instead, by staying receptive and flexible, you can move along the changing tides of life, ready to face any obstacles that come your path. So, how do we apply these principles in life? Lee illustrates,

> "Put water into a cup; it becomes the cup; put water into a bottle; it becomes the bottle."

This highlights the importance of adapting and transforming. Similar to how water takes on the shape of its container, we, too, can adjust to surroundings and circumstances, and instead of trying to run away, we must accept our reality and adapt. Lee emphasises that water can flow smoothly or crash forcefully, and it's ultimately up to us to decide. We hold the power to choose how we tackle life's obstacles. We can opt to go with the flow, welcoming change and growth, or we can resist confronting challenges with reluctance.

We must recognise the patterns influencing our actions to reprogram our thought processes. Whether it pertains to our attire or approach to difficulties, these routines become deeply ingrained through repetition. However, we can bring about lasting transformations by challenging these behaviours and adopting practices.

It is the same as the tree scenarios I shared at the beginning of this section. Visualise watering a tree seed every day, like you would nurture a growing tree – offering it care and attention until it blossoms towards sunlight. This analogy mirrors how we nurture our goals with dedication until they flourish into fruition in our minds.

By picturing, feeling, and confirming our affirmations, we essentially ensure they establish themselves and thrive in our thoughts. This will lead to taking motivated steps towards our goals. I want you to always remember that the journey towards your goals begins in your mind.

So, no matter what stage of life you may be in, plant the seeds of success today and watch as your dreams blossom into reality.

I share these stories with you because I want you to be mindful of your habits and actively try to alter them, which can lead to better changes. By starting with habits, you can gradually shift thought patterns as well. It's crucial to start instilling good habits as early as possible, no matter your age. These habits, whether they involve your health, mindset, or daily routines, will shape who you become over time. The earlier you adopt them, the stronger their impact will be, but it's never too late to start.

Your habits are the foundation of your future, and the sooner you build a solid foundation, the better equipped you'll be to face life's challenges and achieve your goals. Like my friend and mentor Jessen James always says,

> “How you do anything is how you do everything”.

Remember, your future self is shaped by the actions you take today. Looking back on my life, from the vibrant days in Venezuela to the challenging years in Madeira, I see a common thread—a dynamic mindset.

This mindset is not about being perfect; it’s about being adaptable, resilient, and always ready to learn.

NURTURING A DYNAMIC MINDSET THROUGH FIVE KEY HOBBIES

Starting to change your life begins with shifting your mindset. It may seem like a big task, but breaking it down into smaller achievable steps can make a significant difference. One practical approach to enhancing your life involves embracing five hobbies. Each hobby serves a purpose, and collectively, they pave the way towards a harmonious and satisfying existence.

Here's how:

1. A Hobby to Make You Money: This hobby centres around pursuing activities that bring you joy while also offering monetary rewards. It could involve freelancing, investing, crafting goods for sale or launching a business on the side. The essence lies in selecting something that ignites your passion. When you derive joy from what you do, earning money becomes an added bonus rather than an obligation.

2. A Hobby to Keep You Healthy and in Shape: Maintaining an active lifestyle is vital for health and wellness. Whether it's hitting the gym, running, practising yoga or indulging in dance routines, finding an activity that resonates with you is crucial. It's not merely about keeping your body fit; it also contributes to enhancing well-being.

Regular exercise triggers the release of endorphins, promoting happiness and reducing stress levels.

3. A Hobby as a Creative Outlet: Expressing creativity plays a role in our lives. Engaging in a hobby is a way to express ourselves and find comfort. Whether painting, writing, playing an instrument, or cooking, the key is letting your creativity flow without stressing about being perfect.

4. A Hobby to Build Your Knowledge: Another valuable aspect is picking up a hobby that challenges your mind and broadens your knowledge. This could involve reading, learning a new language, taking classes or having enriching conversations. The more you learn, the more you know and the more opportunities you'll notice around you.

5. A Hobby to Evolve Your Mindset: It is crucial to focus on hobbies that help you grow as a person. Activities like meditation, journaling, or practising mindfulness can help you understand yourself better, handle stress effectively, and maintain peace. Developing your mindset involves enhancing self-awareness and resilience.

The thing is, most people know what they want, but I believe almost 90% of them struggle to achieve it because it seems "hard" or "takes time." Adopting the right mindset is essential; although shortcuts may offer wins at times, they rarely lead to sustained success.

Consider the analogy of going to the gym as an example. During January, gyms are bustling with individuals who have set New Year's resolutions to improve their fitness.

However, as the month winds down, many abandon their efforts. Despite starting with enthusiasm, they lose motivation when they don't see progress. I had conversations with some of these people.

A common excuse they gave was being "too busy" with work even though they held 9-to-5 jobs. In contrast, I begin my day at 7 am. and wrap up around 11 pm. I still manage to make time for the gym. It all comes down to priorities and consistent dedication, no matter how small the steps may seem.

Consistency plays a significant role in this. You don't need to dedicate hours every day to each hobby. Even committing 15 to 30 minutes daily can lead to changes over time. The key is to persevere through challenges and stay committed.

As we close the very first chapter, I share my stories to show how the seemingly small moments in life—those rooted in simplicity, family, and hard work—can shape who we become, offering valuable lessons in resilience and growth. The bougainvillea by the gate symbolised resilience, thriving despite its thorns—just like my journey through life. Through these early experiences, I developed a dynamic mindset, continually growing, learning, and evolving.

All these seemingly insignificant moments laid the foundation for resilience and taught me the value of appreciating my surroundings, hard work, and the joy of simplicity. Each challenge was an opportunity for growth, shaping who I am today. In the next chapter, The Rollercoaster of Responsibilities, we'll delve into the demands of growing up.

As I transition from a carefree child to an adolescent, new pressures begin to emerge. This chapter reflects on the complexities of responsibility and how they impact one's development.

Prepare to explore how life's ups and downs build the strength and resilience needed to face adult life head-on.

Be grateful for what you have.

Jessen James

Chapter 2

The Rollercoaster of Responsibility

"Think Twice, Do it Once."

THE ROLLERCOASTER OF RESPONSIBILITY

Life has a way of throwing us into situations that demand more from us than we ever thought we could give. It's in those moments when the weight of responsibility feels overwhelming, and the future seems uncertain that we discover our true strengths. This chapter is about more than just navigating those responsibilities; it's about embracing them, learning from them, and allowing them to shape us into stronger, wiser individuals.

Whether it's the sudden shift from carefree youth to the demands of adulthood, the challenge of balancing health with ambition, or the pressure to provide for those you love, these experiences teach us valuable lessons. They're the moments that test our limits and, in doing so, expand them. This isn't just a chapter in my book; it's a chapter in my life. And maybe it's a chapter in yours, too.

As you read on, you might see glimpses of your own journey, highs and lows, victories and setbacks. And if you do, I hope this chapter offers you insight and encouragement. No matter how wild the ride gets, the rollercoaster of responsibilities is also where we find our most significant growth, profound connections, and, ultimately, the wealthiest rewards.

COSTLY DECISIONS

Two weeks before turning 18, I got married. Now, I know what you're thinking, "so young", right? But for me, it felt like the most natural thing in the world. Love has a way of making things clear, even when everything around you is a blur. One day, I was a teenager worried about what shoes to wear, and the next, I was a husband. It completely changed my life overnight. We didn't waste any time, either.

Shortly after our wedding, we welcomed our child into the world. Holding my baby for the first time, something inside me shifted. There's no other way to describe it. Suddenly, my focus wasn't just on me anymore. Everything I did, every decision I made, had to be for my family. That meant I had to step up in ways I hadn't imagined. One of the first things I did was cut back on drinking. I devoted myself to my family, aiming to give them the best life possible.

The first step was making sure we were financially stable. I worked as many hours as possible, saved every penny, and we had a little cushion within a few months. That's when it hit me. Our family was expanding, and we needed a reliable car. Something safe and spacious but also something I could be proud of. Any man reading you know what I am talking about, right? So, around mid-February 2003, we visited the local dealership. I remember walking in, feeling a mix of excitement and anxiety. The smell of new cars and the glossy sheen of polished metal had me on a high. Then I saw it.

I instantly fell in love with a car. It was ideal—a dark blue Toyota Corolla 1.3 petrol. The colour caught my eye immediately—blue has always been my favourite colour, and this car was the perfect shade. Sleek, reliable, and just the right size, it felt like it was made for me. There was a hitch, though.

As much as I had saved, I didn't have enough funds to buy it outright. I wasn't about to let that stop me, though. After talking it over with my wife, who knew how much this meant to me, we decided to go for it. Therefore, I opted for a loan to bridge the gap. It wasn't an easy choice. Taking on debt felt risky, especially with a new baby and all the other responsibilities piling up. But at the time, I knew it was the right move for our family, and I was confident that this car was worth every penny.

Signing those papers was one of the most nerve-wracking moments of my life. I could feel the weight of every signature, each a commitment to my future and my family's well-being. But at the same time, it felt empowering. I was making a decision, taking control, and doing what needed to be done. Driving off in that car, I felt like I was heading into a new chapter. It was like a tangible sign of progress.

But, almost immediately, the weight of that decision began to press down on me. You see, I had invested all my savings in the payment. The monthly instalments were steep. Additionally, I was the sole breadwinner at home. Every single month's salary felt stretched to the limit.

But you know what? The issue wasn't my income. It was my choice to buy that car. I had enough money to buy a decent car within my means, but I wanted that car. I had let my desire for something better cloud my judgment, and now we were paying the price.

The first few months were the hardest. Every time the payment was due, I felt a pang of anxiety. It was a constant balancing act, ensuring we had enough for groceries, utilities, and all the other little expenses that add up quickly. My wife, bless her heart, tried to be supportive, but I could see the worry in her eyes. We had taken on this burden together, and I couldn't help but feel responsible for the strain it put on us.

Two years flew by in a blur of work, bills, and sleepless nights. We managed to keep our heads above water, but just barely. Each month, I watched as the amount we owed on the car slowly decreased, inching closer to that final payment. I kept reassuring my wife that once we finished paying off this car, things would get better. "Just one more month," I'd say, trying to convince myself as much as her, "Once we're done with the car, we'll have breathing room."

With just one month left before the final payment, I found myself both excited and anxious. We were almost there, free from the burden I had borne for my family. I kept telling myself that everything would improve once we crossed that finish line.

As we inched closer to that final payment, with a feeling of relief and resolve, we thought about starting to save up for a house.

But life has a funny way of throwing curveballs when you least expect it, doesn't it?

One moment, everything is moving along smoothly, and the next, you're hit with something that changes everything. That's exactly what happened to us. I had an accident that resulted in my car, the one we had worked so hard to pay off, was completely wrecked. The worst part wasn't even the car; it was the fact that my wife, who was four months pregnant with our son, and our 2.5-year-old daughter were in the car with me. The stress was overwhelming.

I remember standing on the side of the road, staring at the wreck, the metal twisted and unrecognizable, feeling this surreal mix of shock and disbelief. All I could think about at that moment was, "Thank God we're okay." But still, the weight of what had just happened hit hard. How could this happen now, when we were so close to paying off the car?

To make matters worse, when I finally got the insurance payout, it barely covered a third of what I had invested in the car—excluding the interest. It felt like another punch to the gut, adding insult to injury. I had hoped for a better outcome, but life doesn't always play by the rules. With the limited funds from the insurance, I had to be practical.

So, I went for a more affordable option—a white Fiat Punto 1.0 with six speeds. It wasn't flashy, but it fit my budget, and most importantly, it gave me room to breathe. For the first time in a long while, I didn't have to wake up in the middle of the night stressed about making car payments. There was no more juggling between groceries and gas money or wondering how we'd get by. I started to believe I was in a good place again, financially and emotionally. For a few months, I actually felt like things were finally back on track, so I thought.

Then came the call!

The dealer contacted me, and with that smooth, persuasive tone that only car salesmen seem to perfect, he said, "I have the right car for you; the one you currently have is old." Deep down, I knew that I didn't need a new car, but that voice that always whispers, "Why not?" started getting louder. So, feeling tempted, I visited the dealership," Just to look", I told myself. But you know how that goes. The second I stepped in, I was hooked. The dealer walked me through the features, each one more impressive than the last.

Before I had time to fully process what had happened, I found myself walking into the bank and taking out another loan—this time for double the amount of the first one. And if that wasn't bad enough, it came with a hefty 18% interest rate. At the time, I convinced myself it was the right move.

I kept telling myself I could handle it, that it would all be worth it for a car that made me feel like I was finally getting somewhere. I ended up with a green Toyota Avensis 1.8 petrol. It felt like a symbol of progress like I was moving up in the world. I mean, we've all been there, right? You get something shiny and new, and for a little while, it makes you feel like everything's going to be okay. But deep down, I knew better.

The reality hit hard and fast. It was a terrible decision—a painful, gut-wrenching mistake that quickly proved to be more detrimental than I ever imagined. The payments started piling up, and with that 18% interest rate hanging over me, it felt like I was drowning. The relief I'd felt after buying the Fiat disappeared, and I was back to sleepless nights worrying about how to make ends meet.

Each month felt like a battle as I found myself repeating the same mistake of desiring things beyond my financial capabilities. The enticing promises from the dealer and my cravings pushed us further into debt. The stress crept into every part of my life, straining my family relationships, health, and peace of mind.

Reflecting on those times, I understood the consequences of my actions. The real problem wasn't the car or the money, it was my mindset. The desire for more status, comfort, and validation blinded me to the reality of my situation. I was chasing a dream that wasn't even mine; it was sold to me by a dealer who knew how to prey on my insecurities and desires.

BUY WITH YOUR HEAD, NOT JUST YOUR HEART

In our world, it's easy to get caught up in purchasing things that we truly don't need. People often find themselves spending both their money and time on unnecessary things, and this tendency can begin at a young age.

Allow me to recount a childhood memory that perfectly captures this scenario. During my time in school, my parents had a pragmatic approach when it came to buying things for me. They would provide me with one pencil, eraser, pencil sharpener and ruler that had to last for the school year. Some of my friends had multiples of each item. They often ended up breaking or misplacing them. My parents always said, "If you don't need it, why should we purchase it? You only write with one hand anyway; why would you need two pencils?"

The concept of practicality was instilled in me then, although I didn't fully grasp its importance at the time. Whenever I had some money at hand, I tended to buy whatever caught my eye. One particular memory from when I was 13 years old remains vivid in my mind. I went with my brother to town to shop for new trainers for me. We entered a store named "The Best," which greatly appealed to my brother.

I recall telling him that the shop was too pricey and I only had 14,000 Escudos (€70) to spare. We began searching for a pair of shoes for me.

My brother kept recommending a set of Nike, insisting, "Buy these Nike's. They are nice, and they last long. I have had similar ones for over a year." However, I couldn't fathom spending 9,000 Escudos (€45) on shoes when I typically budgeted under 1,000$ (€5). Then I spotted a pair of roller skates priced at 13,300 Escudos (€66.5), and I instantly fell in love with it. I told my brother, "I'm getting these" He laughed and said, "You don't pay 9000$ (€45) for the trainers, but you will pay 13300 Escudos (€66.5) for the roller skates! That's not going to happen."

Since my brother was older, I couldn't argue too much. I pretended to agree and suggested we go to another shop where I could buy my usual cheap trainers. In the end, I settled for a 600 Escudos (€3) pair. The type that had just broken on me the previous week. Afterwards, we grabbed a drink before my brother headed to school, unaware of my plan. As soon as he rounded the corner, I returned to "The Best" to purchase the roller skates I had fallen in love with.

On that particular Friday, I strutted into school with my new trainers. Come Sunday, our usual football game took place, and guess what? Yes, you guessed right. Unfortunately, the trainers didn't last the day. As for the roller skates, I tried them out four times and quickly realized my lack of skill in using them. They ended up sitting in a corner for 15 years. When I eventually decided to try them again, the wheels were all dry and had fallen apart by the time I was an adult.

Now, you might be thinking, why am I telling you this?

You see, this is just one of many examples of the consumer society we live in. Most of the time, we buy with our hearts, not with our heads. It's easy to get swept up in the excitement of a new purchase without thinking about whether we really need it or if it's a good use of our money.

As I mentioned earlier, it was only later in life that I learned that one of the most powerful sales tactics is to sell emotions. Salespeople understand that if they can evoke feelings in you, you'll buy with your heart, not your head. They offer solutions to your problems and are often the right ones. However, sometimes, they may also convince you to buy things you don't need or bundle unnecessary items together to justify the price they are charging you. It's crucial for us to be mindful of this. The world we live in is constantly pushing us towards consumerism to the point where we feel like slaves to big corporations. By being more aware of our actions and purchases, we can regain control over our lives and money.

Just like I once did, working to make ends meet and paying bills only to find that there was nothing left at the end of the month, I know many people are still facing this struggle today. One of the changes I made was paying attention to every aspect of my life. Being aware and mindful of how you allocate your time and money can truly transform your life. Please take this seriously and maintain discipline. Discipline means sticking to your financial goals consistently, no matter what.

I've seen many people set objectives to save or manage their spending, only to give up shortly after, citing a lack of results. They jump from one strategy to another and then complain they never achieve their financial goals. If you want to see real change in your finances, commit to a plan and follow through with it.

So, how can we shift from being impulsive buyers to making informed and considered choices?

Here are some suggestions:

- Take a moment to reflect before buying: Before splurging on a purchase, take a moment to question whether you genuinely need it. Reflect on whether it will enhance your life, whether it's simply a buy, or whether it will simply gather dust.
- Establish a budget before shopping: Having a defined budget can help you choose what fits your financial capabilities and what priorities to set. I will share some more insights about budgeting later in this chapter.
- Create a shopping list: While out shopping, jot down the items you require and stick to that list. This practice reduces the urge to purchase things.
- Prioritize quality over quantity: At times, it's better to invest a bit more in a high-quality product that lasts longer than opting for alternatives that need frequent replacement. Don't get me wrong; quality does not always mean big brands; sometimes, small brands have excellent quality, too.

- Reflect on past purchases: Take a moment to think about purchases you've regretted in the past. Use these insights to steer your decisions and avoid repeating mistakes.
- Identify emotional triggers: Be aware of what prompts your desire to make a purchase. Are you experiencing excitement, sadness or boredom? Salespeople leverage these emotions. Recognizing your triggers can aid you in making choices.

You see, a dynamic mindset is about more than just thinking on your feet or being flexible. It's about understanding the real cost of your decisions. It's about knowing when to stop and ask yourself, "Why do I want this? What am I really trying to achieve?"

In those moments I shared with you, I had to make important financial decisions, I wasn't thinking about my future or my family. I was thinking about how good it would feel to drive something new, something that made me look successful to others. But success isn't about what you drive, wear, or own. It's about what you can live with and what you can live without. I learned the hard way that sometimes, the things we crave the most are the very things that can lead us down a path of destruction.

As mentioned in my past experiences, that car, that loan, those monthly payments were a symptom of a deeper issue: a mindset that needed to shift.

SHIFTING STRESS TO SUCCESS

Money can be quite a topic for people, causing stress. Embarking on a journey towards a dynamic mindset begins by understanding the significance of your decisions and how they influence your finances, entire life, and loved ones. It involves resisting temptation, finding the quick fix, finding the easy solution, and asking yourself what you truly value. Personally, it took me falling into debt and facing the risk of losing everything to grasp that the price of my desires went beyond money, it affected me emotionally, psychologically and deeply personally.

A dynamic mindset isn't about having more; it's about knowing what you truly need and having the courage to say no to everything else that does not align with your values.

Let's face it: most of the time, the issue isn't about how much we earn but how we manage what we already have. If you were to track every penny you spend, you might be surprised at how much you spend on things that aren't truly essential. In today's society, we are constantly bombarded with messages that require us to consume more. I know that resisting this temptation can be tough, and we buy things that end up unused after one use, cluttering our living spaces. Here's a simple activity to help shift your mindset about money. Take a look around your home and see how many items you own that have not been used in over three months.

Of course, there are exceptions, like seasonal winter and summer clothing, but chances are you'll come across plenty of items that are simply taking up unnecessary space. Therefore, before making a purchase, consider whether you truly need it or if it will just add to your collection of belongings. By adopting this habit, you can reduce your expenses, create breathing room in your home and, most importantly, save money for things that hold value to you.

Consider this: every pound not spent on something is a pound set aside for something better, whether it's an emergency fund, a long-term investment, or that special treat you've been eyeing for some time.

The key is to make mindful decisions about where your money goes.

Earlier, I shared how to make informed choices before any purchase and one practical step is to begin budgeting. While it may seem mundane or confining at first, budgeting can actually be quite liberating. It allows you to track your expenses and make choices about how you allocate your funds.

Budgeting doesn't mean sacrificing enjoyment; it just means you're making sure your money is working for you, not against you.

Here are some tips to kickstart the budgeting process:

- Keep track of your spending: Try jotting down all your monthly expenses. You might be surprised to see where your money is actually going.
- Distinguish between Wants and Needs: Take a look at your list. Categorize each expense as either something you truly need or just something you want. This exercise can help you identify areas where you can cut back.
- Set specific money goals: Determine your goals with your finances, whether it's clearing debt, saving up for a getaway or building an emergency safety net. Having goals is essential.
- Develop a strategy: Create a plan that aligns with your objectives. Prioritize funding necessities first then focus on your goals. Lastly, allocate funds for wants.
- Review and Adapt regularly: Life is unpredictable, so it's essential to revisit your budget and make adjustments as necessary based on changing circumstances.

Ultimately, we all need money; some of us want it more than others, but the need remains universal. It fuels our basic needs, supports our dreams, and often dictates the quality of life we can provide for ourselves and our loved ones.

However, it's easy to get caught up in the pursuit of more, losing sight of the fact that it's not the amount of money you have that truly matters but how you manage it.

By shifting your mindset and being more deliberate in managing your finances, you can reduce stress and gain control over your money matters. Remember, it's not about how much you make but how effectively you manage it that makes the difference. Adopting a mindful approach can turn financial stress into financial success.

MAXIMIZING PRODUCTIVITY

Now that you know how to manage your finances, you also need to manage your time effectively to create a balanced and fulfilling life. Much like money, time is a finite resource, and how you spend it can significantly impact your overall well-being. Just as you track your spending to stay within budget, it's essential to be mindful of how you allocate your hours each day. By managing your time with the same mindfulness you apply to your finances, you can create a more balanced, fulfilling life where both your money and your time work for you, not against you.

Remember, time is the most important asset you have in life. Once it slips away, you can never get it back like you do for money or material possessions. That's why it's crucial to think wisely about how you spend your time so that in a few years, you don't find yourself regretting the things you could have done or the opportunities you let slip away.

I recently came across a powerful concept in a book that made me think: "Imagine you are on your deathbed, and people are saying what you were good at".

This mental exercise serves as an incentive to reflect on how you invest your time. Each day, you are crafting your narrative. So, it is within your control to shape it into something remarkable. Consider the legacy you wish to leave and embrace activities that bring you pride and joy. When you prioritize what truly matters to you, you will begin to lead a life with no regrets. It's about seizing every moment and ensuring that your actions are in line with your values and long-term goals.

You seem everything in life is possible. After I understood this truth, I started to change and improve my story. There's a stark contrast between the start of my journey and where I stand now. I am confident that the chapters in my life I craft going forward will only get better. Embracing improvement is a core belief of mine now, shaping the essence of my existence. If I reunite with a friend after a decade, they will surely see the changes I've undergone. My approach to everything has evolved; even my appearance reflects this change, not due to ageing but because of increased health and vitality.

This transformation is the result of my dedication to personal growth and my deliberate choices regarding how I invest my time.

I'm going to dive into some advanced strategies further down, which is definitely a must-read, so stay tuned!

But let's start with a few practical suggestions that can help you manage your time more effectively right now:

1. Define Clear Objectives: First, you need to know where you're headed. Take a moment to define what you really want to achieve in different areas of your life. Whether it's career goals, personal growth, or something more specific like learning a new skill, clear objectives are your guideposts. They help you decide where to invest your energy, ensuring that your daily actions align with your bigger vision.

2. Prioritize Your Tasks: Here's the thing, not everything on your to-do list is equally important. Focus on the tasks that align with your goals and values. This means sometimes you'll need to say "no" to things that don't serve your growth or happiness—and that's perfectly okay! By focusing on what truly matters, you'll free up time and mental energy to move forward with purpose.

3. Minimize Distractions: We all know how easy it is to get pulled into the social media vortex or distracted by small, unimportant tasks. Instead of letting these distractions steal your time, consider setting boundaries. For instance, you could allocate specific times for social media and stick to them. Use the extra time you save to work towards your goals or enhance your skills—it's incredible how much progress you can make when you eliminate just a few distractions.

4. Reflect Regularly: Life is dynamic, and so are your goals. That's why taking time to reflect on your progress is essential. Are you moving in the right direction? Are there areas where you can adjust your strategy? Regular reflection helps you stay on track and constantly tweak your approach to improve and grow. Think of it like course-correcting as you go—you're steering yourself towards success.

5. Celebrate Achievements: Finally, remember to celebrate the wins, big or small. Reaching milestones, no matter how minor they seem, deserves recognition. Not only does this keep you motivated, but it also reinforces positive habits. Acknowledging your progress is like fuelling the engine—it keeps you going strong!

Remember, no one is responsible for your time apart from you. Time is a commodity that shapes the quality of your life, and guess what? It is you who hold the power to make decisions that pave the way for a purposeful existence. It is time to embrace the journey of improvement in every way and witness how your story unfolds in ways.

Therefore, take control of your time now, focus on what matters the most and make every moment of your life meaningful. I guarantee you that your future self will be grateful. And you know what?

Those in your circle will find motivation in how you live, too!

MASTER YOUR DAY WITH THE 8+8+8 RULE

When maximizing your day, following the 8+8+8 rule can make a difference. This simple approach divides the 24 hours we all have into three segments, allowing for a rounded balance between work, rest and personal life. While following the 8+8+8 rule can help structure your day, I acknowledge that life is not always straightforward. There may be times when you need to adjust your schedule to accommodate priorities. For example, putting in hours on a project might mean sacrificing sleep time – and that's perfectly okay as long as it is not persistent. The goal is to keep the balance as close to the 8+8+8 rule as possible over the long run.

Now, you might be thinking, where do you even begin?

Well, start by assessing how you currently utilize your time during the day. Are you getting rest? Are you allocating time for your loved ones and interests?

Once you understand, strive to reorganize your routine to adhere to the 8+8+8 principle. It may require some effort and fine-tuning. With perseverance, you'll find a balance that works for you.

Remember, it's all about establishing a schedule that empowers you to thrive in every aspect of your life. Let's delve into it more:

8 HOURS OF DEDICATED WORK:

This block of time is reserved for your job or main work tasks, whether in the office, managing your business or working remotely. The focus here is on staying productive and efficient so that you can fully disconnect when transitioning to parts of your day.

8 HOURS FOR RESTFUL SLEEP:

Ensuring you get eight hours of sleep each night is vital for your health and wellness. Quality sleep helps your body recover, boosts your immune system, and enhances your mental clarity. It's important not to compromise on this time needed for your body and mind to rejuvenate.

ALLOCATING 8 HOURS TO THE 3FS, 3HS AND 3SS:

The remaining eight hours are segmented into three categories, each comprising of three components. Let's delve into each:

The 3Fs: Family, Friends and Faith

Family: Spending quality time with family is precious and invaluable in today's busy world, where it often seems like there's never quite enough of it. Let's put it into perspective: if we have just 2 hours and 40 minutes to spend with our family each day, that's a very short time to show our love and care.

This is why it is so important to devote as much time to your loved ones. Whether it involves sharing a meal, discussing your day, or simply enjoying each other's company, spending time with family is essential for nurturing relationships. However, being present means more than being physically there; it means giving them our undivided attention without distractions.

Now, imagine you sitting with your family, sharing laughter and stories while basking in each other's company. Envision relishing these moments without the interruptions of work-related tasks, notifications or the constant urge to glance at your phone. Doesn't that sound great? This is the type of connection we all need.

I have a challenge for you and me. Let's pledge to keep our phones away when spending time with our family. By silencing them, we can resist the temptation to check for messages or alerts. Of course, exceptions can be made for urgent work calls or important matters. However, apart from those instances, let's ensure that our phones do not encroach upon our family time.

I've often observed something that really emphasizes this point. Whenever I dine out with my family, I notice many people at tables engrossed in their phones. They seem preoccupied with social media rather than engaging with the company right in front of them. While social media has its benefits, it can sometimes hinder our social life and interactions. It's quite ironic, don't you think?

We are connected to hundreds of people, yet we fail to establish genuine connections with those physically present.

Don't get me wrong, I am not implying that we should completely abandon social media. It's perfectly acceptable to enjoy it during our leisure time. However, when in the company of family, our focus should be on them and not on our screens. The moments spent with loved ones are priceless and irreplaceable. We should strive to be fully present – listening attentively, engaging in conversation, and relishing every moment.

Therefore, let's commit to being fully engaged with our families during those two hours and forty minutes. Though it may seem like a fraction of our day, it can significantly impact our relationships and overall happiness. Let's set aside our phones and authentically connect with the individuals who hold significance in our lives.

<u>Friends</u>: Cultivating friendships is vital in our lives. Just imagine having 2 hours and 40 minutes dedicated solely to spending time with your friends. You could grab a cup of coffee together, take a walk or engage in activities that friends typically enjoy together. You might also consider using this time to catch up with a friend you haven't seen in a while and have a chat over the phone. The key here is to make sure this time is about your friends because these connections enrich our lives and offer support. Please understand that these are not work-related things or business calls.

Friendship holds great value in our lives. It's worth noting that the five people closest to you often reflect who you are as a person. Your close circle can have an influence on your attitudes, behaviours and overall perspective on life. Therefore, choosing your friends wisely and allocating time for them is crucial.

True friends are the ones who support and inspire us and aren't afraid to point out when we're headed in the wrong direction. They're the ones who give us feedback. While it feels nice to have friends who always praise us for everything we do, there's value in receiving criticism about our mistakes and areas where we can improve. Getting feedback like this can shed light on where we might be slipping up and offer us the chance to make things right and improve.

Consider this: negative feedback isn't always welcome in the business world. However, constructive criticism is what actually propels a business forward and helps it thrive. The same principle applies to our lives. Receiving advice on areas of our lives we could work on from a friend can truly be beneficial. So, when you're hanging out with your friends, treasure those who're willing to speak with you. Appreciate the moments when they uplift you, but value them when they provide criticism. It's finding that balance that strengthens friendships and gives them depth.

Therefore, embrace the 2 hours and 40 minutes you get to spend with your friends.

Focus on being in the moment, enjoying their company, and being open to both positive and constructive feedback. By doing this, you cultivate friendships that not only bring happiness but also push you towards becoming better versions of yourself.

Faith: Faith holds a place in our lives, touching us deeply on a level. The concept of faith can vary among individuals. It may involve practising a religion, meditation, or simply taking moments to reflect on your beliefs and values. Whatever you believe in, faith can offer guidance and solace in your life.

No matter how busy you are, you have 2 hours and 40 minutes each day to nurture your faith. I use this time to set and reflect on goals, take walks in nature, meditate or engage in activities that bring me closer to myself. For a while, I didn't grasp the significance of jotting down my goals; it felt like a task.

However, once I began this practice, I noticed significant changes in my life. Putting goals into writing makes them real and provides guidance, even if you think you don't need it. Since then, dedicating time daily to focus on my goals has become a habit.

Meditation was another practice I underestimated until I committed to it for 30 minutes every day.

There are so many benefits of meditation, here are a few:

- Improved concentration: Meditation clears the mind for better task focus.
- Emotional well-being: Meditation fosters a positive mindset.
- Enhanced self-awareness: Through meditation, you can gain deeper insight into your thoughts and emotions.
- Promotes emotional health: Meditation aids in managing stress and anxiety, contributing to improved health.
- Improved quality of sleep: Engaging in meditation can enhance the quality of your sleep.
- Increased creativity: A peaceful, clear mind is more receptive to ideas and creative thinking.

Meditation proves advantageous for all aspects of life. It serves as a tool for development and self-empowerment. Instituting change within yourself is crucial to instigate change in your life. Meditation facilitates this process, making it smoother and quicker. Whether it involves setting and assessing goals, taking walks in nature, or practising meditation, these activities aid in connecting with yourself. They offer clarity, purpose, and a sense of tranquillity.

Hence, wisely utilising those two hours and forty minutes is vital. Integrate them into your routine. Write down your goals and review them regularly. Dedicate time to meditation and relish the benefits it brings. Embrace this time as sacred to you; you'll discover that navigating through life's trials and transitions becomes more manageable.

The 3Hs: Health, Hygiene and Hobby

Health: Health is the foundation of everything we do. This encompasses activities such as exercising, maintaining a diet, and tending to your mental well-being. Staying physically active and fuelling your body with food are important aspects of your life.

Picture having 2 hours and 40 minutes daily dedicated solely to looking after your well-being. For me, this time is reserved for hitting the gym, swimming, eating healthy meals and attending; occasionally, it is for routine check-ups with my doctor. Prioritizing your health is a crucial self-care act for yourself and those dear to you.

Consider this scenario when onboarding an aeroplane; the flight attendants always advise passengers to secure their oxygen masks before assisting others. This is because if you run out of oxygen, you won't be able to help anyone else. The same principle applies to your health. If you're not healthy, you won't be able to achieve your goals, enjoy life, or support your family and friends. One day, a wise man said,

> "Eat your food as your medicine, otherwise, you have to eat medicine as your food. The one who loves you will never leave you for another because, even if there are 100 reasons to give up, they will find a reason to hold on."

The essence of this saying lies in the fact that consuming foods can potentially reduce one's reliance on medications in the future. A balanced diet rich in fruits, vegetables, lean proteins, and whole grains plays a role in preserving overall well-being. It is advisable to limit intake of sugar, salt, and unhealthy fats for health maintenance.

Engaging in activity is essential for maintaining good health. Whether you prefer hitting the gym, swimming or simply walking, staying active helps keep your body fit and your mind alert. Choosing an exercise routine that you find enjoyable is vital to ensure consistency. Regular visits to your healthcare provider are also an aspect of looking after your well-being.

These check-ups can detect health issues, making them easier to manage. Don't wait until you feel unwell before seeing a doctor; proactive check-ups play a role in maintaining health. Always remember that dedicating around 2 hours and 40 minutes daily to prioritize your health can impact your well-being.

Focus on consuming foods, engaging in physical activity, and keeping up with medical appointments. Remember, taking care of yourself first allows you to better care for others. Your health is your most valuable asset, so treat it with the importance it deserves.

Hygiene: You know, personal hygiene is one of those things we all agree is essential. Sometimes, we must remember to give it the attention it deserves. Daily practices like showering, brushing your teeth diligently, and grooming contribute significantly to feeling good about yourself and promoting health. Hygiene goes beyond smelling and looking clean; it's about maintaining our health, too. Neglecting hygiene can pose health risks.

Let's delve into the Fundamentals of Personal Hygiene a bit more, shall we?

First and foremost, personal hygiene entails more than taking a shower. While showering is crucial, there's a lot more to it. Regular showers are essential for washing away dirt, sweat and bacteria that build up on our skin. Brushing your teeth helps prevent breathing and dental problems, but think about the impact of having great teeth on your confidence.

Some people sometimes forget the little but essential things like handwashing. It's important to wash your hands after using the restroom, before meals and after being around sick individuals. You might be wondering why I'm writing this. But trust me, the most educated and clean people sometimes forget, and of course, I don't want to start talking about the impact it had when we went through the pandemic. This also applies to trimming your nails, as long nails can trap dirt and bacteria, potentially causing infections.

Now, going beyond the basics, let's touch upon one often overlooked aspect: skincare. Taking care of your skin is vital for health as skin is our biggest organ. In the past, I believed that basic hygiene practices were sufficient. Just a shower and brushing my teeth seemed enough.

However, as time passed, I came to realize that neglecting my skin health and not using protection at work was an oversight. Now, I'm dealing with marks on my face and body as a result of it.

The lack of protection, such as Personal Protective Equipment (PPE) while working, has exposed me to dust and other irritants that have caused damage to my skin.

You see, maintaining hygiene goes beyond avoiding unpleasant odours or looking presentable; it is crucial, for overall health. Maintaining hygiene is essential to prevent infections, illnesses and long-term harm to your skin and overall health. While hygiene may appear uncomplicated it's easy to overlook the steps that can have an impact.

Trust me—taking care of your skin, hair and overall cleanliness is well worth it.

Hobby: Hobbies are activities that we do purely for fun and enjoyment, which can bring much richness to our lives. Hobbies can involve engaging in activities you enjoy and find relaxing as a way to unwind. These could involve reading, gardening, painting, or playing an instrument.

I've had a journey with my hobbies over the years. Let me share some highlights. Between 2008 to 2012, I discovered my love for electronics and robotics. I spent hours tinkering with circuits, creating robots, and delving into the inner workings of these amazing machines. There were times when I'd get so engrossed in my projects that time seemed to slip. Looking back now, I can say without a doubt that every moment was well worth it. The satisfaction of building something from scratch and witnessing it come alive was beyond words.

Between 2012 and 2015, I took a leap into programming. I immersed myself in learning Java and HTML during this period. While I had a grasp of it then, it's safe to say that my skills are a bit rusty now. If you were to ask me to write a simple method, "Hello, World!" program today, I might find myself struggling with it! During that period, programming was a pastime that really challenged my mind and helped me grow my skills.

Since 2015, I've been deeply involved in researching investments in property. I enjoy delving into market trends seeking out opportunities and making informed choices.

Additionally, I take pleasure in attending networking events related to business and property. These activities not only bring me happiness, but also play a role in my personal and professional development.

Hobbies don't necessarily have to align with your job or business. However, believe me when I say they can significantly enhance your work experience when you're able to derive enjoyment, from them while also gaining benefits.

Here's why hobbies hold power:

- Stress Relief: Engaging in activities you're passionate about can significantly reduce stress levels and enhance your quality of life.
- Skill Enhancement: Pursuing hobbies often involves acquiring skills that can be rewarding and beneficial across areas of life.
- Boosting Creativity: Many hobbies create creativity, which can positively impact your endeavours by encouraging innovative thinking.
- Networking Opportunities: Involvement in hobby-related gatherings can lead to connections and meaningful friendships.
- Discovering Your Interests: If you need help deciding which hobby to pursue, consider these suggestions to help you find one that resonates with you.
- Reflect on Your Passions: Take a moment to think about what brings you joy during your leisure time. What activities captivate your attention and make time fly by?

- Experiment with New Activities: Embrace the opportunity to try out hobbies. You may stumble upon an enthusiasm that surprises you.
- Engage with a Community: Explore clubs or online groups that align with your interests. Being part of a community can enrich your hobby experience and help you maintain your motivation.
- Allocate Time: Carve out moments each week for your hobby. Prioritizing activities that bring happiness is essential for well-being.

As you can see, engaging in hobbies goes beyond distractions; they play a role, in maintaining our mental and emotional well-being. Pursuing your hobbies can bring satisfaction. It could even boost your professional path. Just one thing, though: while immersing yourself in hobbies is fulfilling, it's crucial to strike a balance with your responsibilities.

A few simple things you can consider are defining time slots for pursuing your hobbies and ensuring consistency in following them. This approach prevents neglecting duties. You can also seek ways to seamlessly integrate your hobbies into life without overwhelming yourself with commitments.

One last thing I want to leave you with is adaptability, which is key. There may be instances where adjusting your hobby schedule becomes necessary due to obligations. Remember, maintaining equilibrium between aspects of life is vital.

THE 3SS: SOUL, SERVICES AND SMILE

Soul: Now, let's dive into the first "S": the soul. The concept of the soul is deeply rooted in various spiritual and philosophical traditions. What the soul is and what we can do to nurture it varies depending on cultural, religious, and personal beliefs. But one thing is clear: taking care of your soul is vital for a fulfilling life. Many spiritual traditions emphasize the important of nurturing and cultivating the soul.

This is your time to connect with something greater, may it be a higher power, the universe or your inner self, nourish your soul with activities that bring you happiness and fulfilment. This might include:

- Engage in meditation by sitting and focusing on your breath. Allow your thoughts to pass without judgment. Meditation aids, in discovering peace and mental clarity.
- Connect with your power through prayer. Express gratitude, seek guidance. Simply share your thoughts and emotions.
- Engage in self-reflection by taking a moment to contemplate your day, actions and emotions. What insights have you gained? How can you evolve?
- Experience fulfilment through acts of service. Whether volunteering, assisting a friend or performing a kind gesture for a stranger, helping others can be profoundly rewarding.

These practices can promote spiritual growth, inner peace, and a deeper connection to yourself and others. Some believe that expanding one's knowledge and wisdom can enrich the soul. This can involve studying texts, philosophy, and science and engaging in lifelong learning to gain a deeper understanding of the world and ourselves. Simply put, never stop learning. Whether it's a new skill, hobby, or information, keep your mind active and curious.

Engaging in meaningful activities that align with your values and contribute to the well-being of others is often seen as a great way to nourish the soul. Living within your values makes you feel more authentic and fulfilled. It is believed to strengthen the soul and lead to greater spiritual fulfilment. Honesty, integrity, humility, and kindness are some of my values. I will be sharing more on the next part, services.

Love and compassion are often regarded as essential qualities of the soul. By cultivating these qualities for yourself and others, you can experience greater harmony, happiness, and spiritual growth. This will allow you to treat yourself with the same kindness and compassion you would offer a dear friend. Self-love involves recognizing your worth and taking care of your physical, emotional, and mental health.

Furthermore, you will also be able to better understand and empathize with others' struggles and joys. As a result, you will be able to be there for them in meaningful ways, offering support, encouragement, and understanding.

Ultimately, what you can do to their soul is a deeply personal and subjective matter, influenced by their beliefs, values, and experiences. It's essential to explore and engage with practices that resonate with you and align with your understanding of the nature of the soul.

This journey of nurturing your soul is a unique and individual one, and it's essential to find what works best for you.

<u>Services</u>: You can allocate 2 hours and 40 minutes for services. What I mean is part of this time can be spent helping the community, including friends and family. It's about making small gestures that have a significant impact, and it's something everyone can do.

You don't need to perform grand acts to create a big impact, it's all about the small gestures. You may be surprised how everyday small actions can be incredibly powerful. Giving back to others through volunteering or acts of kindness can be incredibly rewarding.

This reminds me of Jessen James when he said,

> "Go out there and give back"

Here are some examples:

- Helping someone: Extend a helping hand by helping them cross the street or carry their belongings. Such simple acts of kindness can truly brighten their day.

- Charity work: Getting involved with organizations can positively influence the community. Whether serving meals at a shelter, coordinating donations, or participating in fundraising events, your contribution is meaningful.

- Supporting Daily Activities: Volunteer to assist your neighbours or friends with their tasks. This could involve anything from tending to the garden to looking after children or running errands.

- Providing Mentorship to Those in Need: Share your wisdom and expertise with someone who could benefit from it. Whether it's an individual or a peer your guidance can have an impact.

I have some habits that might seem quirky to others, but they stem from the values my parents instilled in me. For instance, when I see a fridge open in the supermarket, I close it all the time. It's a small action, but it saves energy and keeps food fresh. When I see a piece of paper on the floor, I always pick it up and put it into the bin.

Sometimes people say I have a thing or two wrong in my head because they don't see anyone else doing stuff like this. And my response?

Yes, I may have one or two things wrong in my head, but I cannot forget the values my parents taught me, which everyone else seems to have forgotten already. My grandmother used to say,

> "Education starts at home, and it will go everywhere with you. You can see the education others have at home if you pay attention to what they do outside"

I heard this time and time again, and it stuck with me. So many times, when I see people throwing rubbish on the floor, I imagine their house must be a mess. If everyone were responsible and did their duties as a good citizen, the world would be a very different place. As you can see, serving others involves putting into action the beliefs that's important to us and striving to improve the world every day in small ways. It's essential to recognize that even the tiniest gestures can create an impact and that our commitment to these principles can motivate others.

Through engaging in these acts of kindness, we play a part in fostering a kinder, more considerate and united global community.

Smile: A smile is a universal language of kindness and joy :)! It has the power to brighten someone's day, uplift spirits, and create a sense of warmth and connection.

So, here is a smile to you!

Remember, no matter what you are going through, a smile can be a simple yet powerful gesture that spreads positivity and happiness.

When we are a kid, we be always smiling to everyone without a second thought. It did not matter if we knew them; we just smiled. It's a natural part of our innocence and joy. But when we grow up, our minds become cluttered with worries and responsibilities, and sometimes, even if someone smiles at us, we might take it the wrong way. But it is even more impactful to put aside whatever we are going through and be the first ones smiling at others. You never know how much someone might need that little bit of positivity.

Smiling can make someone's day better, and it can make us feel good, too.

I remember when I was working as a chef in the kitchen, there was a lady who was the customer services manager, and she used to say to me all the time, "Come on, Manuel, smile!". I'd try for a few seconds, but then I'd get busy with the food and my smile would disappear again.

However, I always smiled at the customers as it was an open kitchen and I could see them. But when I was working my concentration kept me from smiling.

After a few months, the lady came and told me,

"I have been at the bar watching your guys working, and I felt like I had to tell you this: I don't know why, but today you are smiling. Are you ok?"

And I said, "Yes, leaving the dream, and now I understand why you are always telling me to smile. Thank you".

To my surprise, she said, "No, I'm the one who has to say thank you."

That moment was a reminder of how powerful a simple smile can be. It's not just about brightening someone's day; it also has the ability to uplift our own spirits and create a sense of connection and joy within us. Smiling doesn't just change others' perceptions of us; it also impacts our feelings.

So, I urge you to make it a daily practice to smile, no matter how busy or stressed you are. If you find it hard to, take time for activities that make you smile and bring joy into your life. Whether it's watching a movie, spending time with pets, or anything else that lifts your spirits. It may seem like small a gesture, but its effects are substantial.

Whether you're sharing a smile with a stranger passing by, a coworker in the office or a friend, always remember that you're spreading happiness and warmth, and the best part is that it doesn't cost you anything. Keep Smiling and watch as that positivity radiates outwards into the world.

KEEP SMILING!

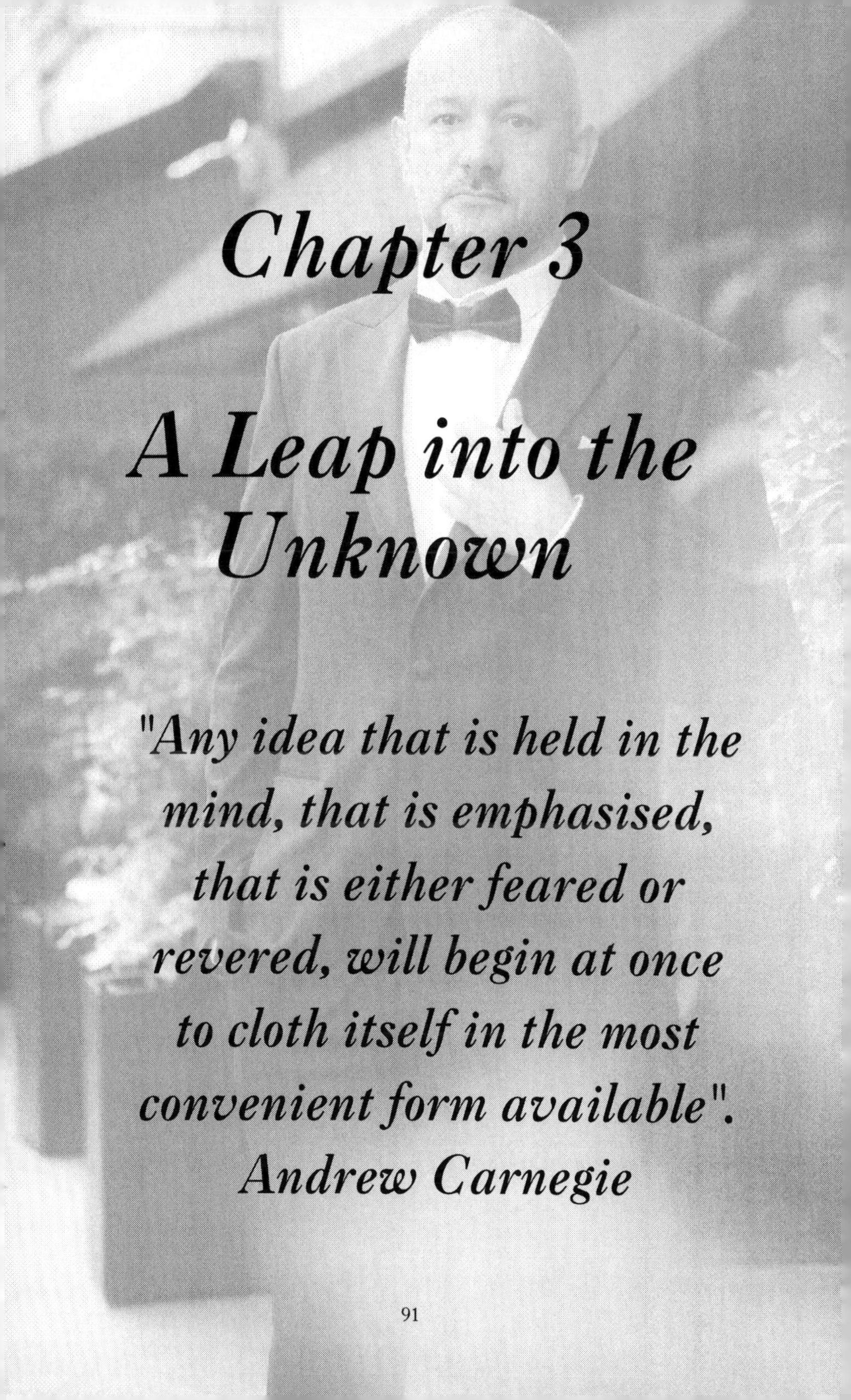

Chapter 3

A Leap into the Unknown

"Any idea that is held in the mind, that is emphasised, that is either feared or revered, will begin at once to cloth itself in the most convenient form available".

Andrew Carnegie

A LEAP INTO THE UNKNOWN

Change is never easy, and we often resist it, especially when everything feels familiar and safe. But sometimes, life pushes us in unexpected directions, forcing us to confront our fears and take bold steps forward. In 2008, I found myself standing at the edge of a new chapter, torn between the comfort of what I knew and the uncertainty of what was to come.

In this chapter, I want to take you on a journey through one of the most pivotal moments in my life—the decision to leave my beloved Madeira, my home, and everything familiar behind to start a new life in the UK. It wasn't just a physical move; it was a shift in mindset, a leap into the unknown that would change everything for me and my family.

Now, you might be thinking, why is this story important?

It is because we all face moments when we must make tough decisions, where the path ahead isn't clear, but staying still isn't an option. It's in these moments that we discover who we truly are. Leaving behind the security of my island home to chase a better future wasn't just about survival—it was about growth, about learning to trust myself and embrace change even when it felt overwhelming.

I believe everyone can relate to the lessons I learned during this time: perseverance, resilience, and the courage to step out of your comfort zone. This chapter isn't just about my story—it's about the power we all have to rewrite our narratives, even when life throws unexpected challenges our way.

So, let's go back to 2008, when it all began—a time of hope, fear, and the unknown.

MY FLIGHT FROM FAMILIARITY

There I was, standing at the edge of my beloved Madeira, a piece of heaven nestled in the vast Atlantic Ocean. Living in Madeira was like experiencing a unique blend of beauty and barriers. Confused? Let me explain.

With its dramatic cliffs, lush green valleys, and vibrant culture, the scenery created a setting straight out of a postcard. But when it came to career prospects, it felt like hitting a roadblock. The mentality there was stuck in the past, emphasising status and competition, overgrowth and progress. It felt like I was living in a world that lagged ten years behind, where success was measured by one's ego rather than their character's depth.

Madeira was my home, and I loved it deeply. The island was alive with traditions, a close-knit community, and a rhythm of life that felt safe and predictable.

Yet, this predictability began to feel like a chain holding me back from the life I yearned for. The social circles I moved into were often steeped in comparison and rivalry. Friends were more interested in outdoing each other than in personal growth or collective advancement. There was a sense of smallness, a ceiling that I kept bumping my head against, and I knew, deep down, that I needed to break free. I love the saying,

> "You are not a tree; move."

Our minds aren't fixed like a tree rooted in one spot; they're more akin to muscles that require exercise. The more we challenge ourselves to think differently and venture beyond our comfort zones, the more robust and resilient our mindset becomes. I realised that life's journey is much like toning your muscles at the gym; it requires constant effort, dedication, and, most importantly, a dynamic mindset.

So, if you feel confined by your surroundings or others' expectations, always remember that you have the ability to break free. You hold the power to shape a life that speaks to your innermost being to pursue your goals and dreams. It all begins with shifting your mindset, embracing the unknown, and having faith in your capacity to thrive.

Looking back, I am glad I did.

Leaving Madeira was a challenging decision. I was leaving behind everything I had known—my family, friends, and familiarity with my island home. But the thought of staying and not growing was far more terrifying. I yearned to build a life on my terms, so with nothing but a backpack full of aspirations and a heart brimming with optimism, I embarked on a journey that would take me far from the familiar sights and sounds of Madeira.

My brother, who had always been my silent supporter, helped me pay for the flight for me and my family, as I didn't have enough. It was a mix of emotions: excitement, fear, and sadness, but somewhere deep within, I knew it was the right decision.

As the plane soared across the azure sky, Madeira slowly disappeared from my view. It was a bittersweet moment, watching the place that had shaped so much of who I was slipping away, knowing I was leaving behind the comfort of everything I had ever known. Yet, with every mile that passed beneath us, I could feel the distance growing physically and emotionally between me and the life I had once led.

There was an undeniable sense of possibility in the air, a rush of excitement that pulsed through my veins. The future stretched out before me like an open road, full of unknown twists and turns, and for the first time in a long while, I felt truly alive. It was as if the sky was whispering promises of new beginnings, urging me into this next chapter of my life.

This wasn't just about changing my location; it was about changing my life, seizing every opportunity that came my way and crafting a life that was uniquely my own.

But even as I felt the thrill of what was to come, a quiet undercurrent of worry tugged at the edges of my mind. This journey wasn't just about me; I had two young children, just six and three years old, who were counting on me. The weight of that responsibility was enormous. I was leaving behind not just the familiarity of Madeira but also the network of family and friends who had always been there to support me.

How would I manage in a foreign country with no safety net and no one to lean on? The questions circled in my mind, but I pushed them aside. I knew this move was necessary for them as much as for myself.

The thought of my children, with their wide-eyed innocence and boundless energy, gave me strength. They were my world, and I was determined to provide them with a life full of possibilities, to show them that we can pursue dreams and overcome challenges. I wanted them to grow up knowing their father was brave enough to step into the unknown and take risks for a better future. The road ahead was unknown, but as the plane continued its journey, I felt ready to take that first step into the future.

A future that was mine to create, full of possibilities, with my children by my side.

So, I found myself fresh off the plane in the UK, excited while embarking on a new chapter in my life. On that day, standing at the airport gate with my luggage ready and my heart racing, I could feel it reverberating throughout my entire being. Freshly graduated with qualifications in engineering and electronic engineering, I was convinced that these degrees would pave the way for a future ahead. I had worked tirelessly, pouring hours upon hours into my studies, sacrificing sleep, leisure time and even a bit of my sanity to reach this point. I had dreams as vast as the sky I was about to fly through and an ironclad belief that I was destined for greatness.

I stepped out of the airport, taking in the cool, crisp air that tasted of opportunity and adventure. I could already see the life I would build—the job offers that would roll in, the projects I would lead, and the people I would impress with my skills. It was all there in my mind, vivid and vibrant, waiting to be painted into reality.

LANGUAGE BARRIER

Moving to England was a massive step for me. When I arrived, I didn't know a word of English. It felt like starting from scratch all over again. This time, it took me longer to grasp the language. Interestingly, I didn't forget Portuguese or Spanish, the languages I already knew. This made me reflect on how we pick up languages as adults compared to when we're young.

Have you ever observed a child learning a language?

As I mentioned in Chapter 1, seeing how they absorb everything effortlessly, like a sponge, is fascinating. Learning happens naturally for them. As adults, it's a different story. Our minds are no longer slates. Learning a language as an adult is about building upon our existing knowledge. It's similar to enhancing the capabilities of a system that's already in place.

Our brain integrates the language with what we already know. It's not about starting over from scratch; it's more about broadening and honing our skills. Indeed, it may take longer for adults to achieve fluency in a language. However, that doesn't mean it's unattainable. In reality, there are ways for adults to learn. We have access to resources that draw upon life experiences, and we possess a deeper understanding of how languages function.

Let me give you an example. Picture a child encountering the word "boat". They might spot a toy boat floating in the bathtub. Gradually comprehend that this object is referred to as a "boat." They create an image of what a boat looks like while linking it with the word they learned. When comparing this to an adult learning a language, it's different from a child's experience.

Adults already have a mental image of what a boat looks like and have perhaps even been on boats before.

So, they don't have to start from scratch when they come across the word "boat" in a language. Instead, they relate the word to the concept they already possess.

It's similar to constructing connections across languages and establishing routes for communication and comprehension, just like installing an app on your phone. You don't need to reset the device; you simply download and incorporate the app into the existing system.

This process is like rewriting a piece of code. We're not starting from a blank slate but modifying and updating the program. Children take their image of a boat and assign it a new label by associating it with the word in the newly acquired language. Thus, in their minds, one object exists, a boat with two names: one in the native language and one in the language being learned. Likewise, as adults learn words, they add them to their vocabulary without removing or replacing what they already know. The ability to link words with concepts is what gives adult language learning its potency.

I was lucky that my first job didn't require much speaking. My wife and I had a position lined up at a café in Gatwick, where we were set to clean tables. It was a nice start for us, especially since my sister helped us secure those jobs before moving to the UK. Our lives were a juggling act of epic proportions for the first three months. My wife started work at 2 am and finished at 2 pm, while I worked from 2 pm to 1 am.

We hardly saw each other. Our kids became our relay baton, passed from one parent to the other in a flurry of "Hi" and "Bye" at Gatwick airport. I'd take the kids to the airport, wait for her to finish, hand them over, and then rush off to my shift. When I finished, the taxi that would bring me home was taking her to work. It was a gruelling schedule, and we only had one day off a week, Thursday.

While everyone else looked forward to Sunday, our little family lived for Thursdays. Despite our challenges, we managed pretty well, living in our own little bubble of contentment.

However, it wasn't long before that bubble began to deflate. Just three months into my job, the café closed its doors unexpectedly, leaving us in a precarious situation and forcing us to confront the reality of our circumstances. I had imagined that my qualifications as an electrician and electronic engineer would speak for themselves and that employers would see the potential in my expertise and welcome me with open arms.

The qualifications that had once felt like a golden ticket to success were now like a weight around my neck, dragging me down as I struggled to find my footing in this foreign land.

But I couldn't give up. Giving up was never an option, especially with my family depending on me.

I had big dreams and high hopes. That's how it's supposed to be, right? You work hard, earn your qualifications, and suddenly, life hands you the key to success on a silver platter?

But life, as it turned out, had other plans in store for me.

In my home country, we were taught English in schools, but it was more of a formality, a subject we had to pass to move on to the next grade. We memorised grammar rules, recited vocabulary lists, and filled in the blanks in our textbooks. But real, living, breathing English—the kind you needed to navigate life in the UK was something I had never fully grasped.

Sure, I could read technical manuals and understand diagrams, but when it came to holding a conversation, asking for directions, or, heaven forbid, cracking a joke, I was completely out of my depth.

Therefore, having certification as an electrician and engineer didn't count much when you struggled to put a sentence in English. Employers didn't just want someone who could wire a circuit or fix an electronic system; they wanted someone who could communicate, collaborate, and understand the nuances of their language and culture. And at that time, that person wasn't me.

THE ELECTRIFYING CHEF

Shortly after the café closed, my wife and I found ourselves in a tough situation. The company we worked for had a position open at a restaurant, but only one of us could stay. My wife and I had applied for the chef role, and we were hoping we could both keep working. However, the restaurant manager pulled me aside one day and said, "We can keep one of you in the restaurant, but the other will have to go home and look for a job."

It was a tough blow. We needed both incomes, especially with two young children to care for, but with the economy in shambles, finding another job wasn't going to be easy. After a long conversation, my wife and I made the difficult decision: I would take the chef position, and she would search for another job. Her English was much better than mine, and we figured she'd have a better chance of finding something else while I could hold down the fort at the restaurant.

At the time, it seemed like the best plan.

But 2008 was brutal, especially with the financial crisis looming over us. My wife's job search turned into a year-and-a-half-long struggle. Despite her qualifications and determination, she faced rejection after rejection. It was disheartening to watch her fight so hard without success, knowing how capable she was. We had hoped it would only take a few months, but the job market was unforgiving.

Finally, after what felt like an eternity, she landed a position as a food runner—ironically, at the same restaurant where I was working. It wasn't ideal, far from what she deserved, but it was something. We were grateful for it because at least we had two incomes again, and that was crucial with bills piling up and mouths to feed.

So, I worked as a chef in a restaurant at Gatwick Airport. And, yes, you read that right: I, the guy who knew more about circuits and wires than spices and sauces, ended up cooking in a kitchen. And you know what? It was a humbling experience. I transitioned from doing domestic and commercial eclectics to the chaotic art of cooking. It was like being "lost in translation," but in the best possible way. And you know what?

I embraced it wholeheartedly.

When life hands you lemons, they say, make lemonade. But why stop at lemonade? Add some zest and some honey, and make it your own.

Working as a chef taught me more about life than any book or lecture ever could. I learned the value of dedication, of showing up day after day, even when the going gets tough. And believe me, working under pressure was the norm, as the restaurant was most of the time bustling. We had to craft amazing dishes under stress, and that constant literal and figurative heat built my perseverance.

I didn't just learn to face adversity; I thrived in the midst of it when the chaos of the kitchen seemed to melt away any lingering doubts. It also taught me the importance of communication: how to shout instructions over the clattering of pans and make yourself heard when everything around you is chaotic and loud. Over time, I began to see my journey in a new light. Every challenge, every rush hour, was a lesson in resilience.

You see, life didn't hand me the key to success on a silver platter, but it gave me something even better: a chance to discover who I am and to find my true passion. It wasn't the life we had envisioned when we left Madeira, but we made it work. I came to the UK as an electrician, but I found myself as a chef.

And in the process, I learned that sometimes, the path to success isn't a straight line. It's a winding road full of unexpected turns and challenges. But if you keep moving forward and open your heart to new possibilities, you'll find the journey is the real reward. So here I am, The Electrifying Chef, proof that life's detours can lead to the most unexpected and beautiful destinations.

And if there's another thing I've learned, it's this:

> “Success isn't about where you end up;
> it's about the journey that gets you there.”

Sometimes, the most valuable life lessons come from the most unexpected places. They come from the moments when you're out of your element and forced to adapt, learn, and grow. And that's what a dynamic mindset is all about. Embrace the twists and turns, the detours that take you off the beaten path. You never know where they might lead you or what they might teach you along the way.

And in the end, that's what matters, not the destination, but the journey and the person you become because of it.

YOUR INNER VOICE

Have you ever found yourself standing in the middle of a bustling kitchen wondering, "Is this really what I'm meant to be doing?" That was me every single day for five years. Some days, I indulged in making the perfect English breakfast, and sometimes, Mexican delights in the kitchen, questioning my life choices. But despite the joy I found in creating beautiful meals, there was a nagging feeling inside me that I couldn't quite ignore—a small, persistent voice that whispered, "There's more to life than this."

It wasn't that being a chef wasn't fulfilling. I loved the adrenaline rush of a busy kitchen, the satisfaction of a well-executed dish, and the smiles on people's faces when they took that first bite. But deep down, I knew there was something more I was meant to do, something beyond just fulfilling someone else's culinary dreams.

Have you ever felt that inner voice nudging you, urging you to step beyond your comfort zone?

It's easy to dismiss it, to chalk it up to fleeting dissatisfaction or a passing thought. But the truth is, that voice is there for a reason. It's a guide, pointing you toward your true potential and challenging you to explore uncharted territories. When that inner voice insisted that I could do more, I realised I had to listen. You see, a dynamic mindset allows you to see beyond the present moment. It reminds you that where you are today doesn't define where you'll be tomorrow.

So, I did what seemed rational at the time. I took a leap of faith, traded my chef's jacket for a hard hat, and ventured into the world of engineering.

Every experience, even the ones that make you question your path, is shaping you for what's to come. The kitchen wasn't my final stop—it was just another step in my journey of evolution. Looking back, I realise now that those moments of doubt were part of a much bigger journey—a necessary step in evolving my career and mindset. You see, a dynamic mindset isn't just about being flexible or adapting to change.

It's about constantly challenging yourself to think beyond your current circumstances. It's about understanding that growth isn't always linear and that sometimes, what feels like stagnation is actually a quiet period of transformation.

Come January 2013, I plunged headfirst into the world of entrepreneurship. The year started with the usual whispers of New Year's resolutions, promises I made that this would be the year I finally broke free from the grind and started something of my own. I had no real plan, no clear vision, just the stubborn belief that I could figure it out as I went along. For nine months, I worked three days a week, Friday, Saturday, and Sunday, at Gatwick, and I spent the remaining days, from Monday to Thursday, building my business. It was a grind, a constant juggle between two demanding worlds, but deep down.

It wasn't all smooth sailing, as I was completely unaware of the challenges ahead. It was about burning the midnight oil, getting up at dawn, and dealing with stress levels higher than a tripped circuit breaker. That was my life. But still, I was determined to make it work.

I dedicated myself entirely to my new venture, working harder than before and guess what? But as the weeks turned into months, that excitement started to fade, and reality hit me like a ton of bricks.

After four months, though, I found myself buried in paperwork. What had started as a bold venture into entrepreneurship quickly turned into a daily struggle, just another job (just over broke), and not a particularly rewarding one. It wasn't a calculated move to grow my business; it was sheer desperation.

The work was hard, the hours were long, and the payoff was... well, let's say I was barely scraping by. There were days I'd look in the mirror and barely recognise the person staring back at me. I was supposed to be the boss, the visionary, the one with all the answers. Instead, there were moments when I questioned my decisions, unsure if I had made the right choices. The persistent inner voice that had once encouraged me now seemed to question my every move. "Why are you here?" it asked. "Is all this effort truly worthwhile?"

Every day felt like a battle. I was lost in a maze of challenges I wasn't equipped to handle. I had no clue how to find customers, let alone keep them. Pricing for me was a mystery. I was either overcharging and scaring people away or undercharging and digging myself deeper into a financial hole. Sales skills? Well, non-existent. Marketing? Not a chance. Business knowledge? I was winging it every step of the way. And research? Who had time for that when I struggled to keep the lights on?

To make matters worse, I found myself doing electrical jobs for people who either didn't pay or took their sweet time doing so. It wasn't just about the money, though it was a big part. It was the feeling of being undervalued, of pouring my time and energy into work, that no one seemed to appreciate. I worked with a few people here and there, but it felt like I was on my own most of the time.

When I was working at the restaurant or working for anybody else, it may not have been fulfilling, but at least there was a clear roadmap and guidance for the job. But I needed direction or support tools to navigate into the territory, and I needed direction and a roadmap. I felt lonely and lost.

It would have been easy to throw in the towel, to retreat back to the familiarity of the kitchen. But something kept me going. That inner voice that used to whisper had become a roar, telling me that this journey was about more than just building a business. It was about proving to myself that I was capable of more and that I had the potential to create something beyond food.

And that's the thing about listening to your inner voice; it's not always about finding immediate success or making the right choices every time. It's about growth, about pushing yourself to explore the limits of what you can achieve.

Looking back now, I realise that those struggles were my real education. They forced me to learn, adapt, and grow in ways I never would have if everything had gone smoothly. So, if you ever question your path and feel that there might be something more out there for you, don't ignore that feeling. That inner voice is your compass, guiding you toward your true purpose. Listen to it, trust it, and have the courage to follow where it leads.

FROM SPARKS TO PIPES

One afternoon at the beginning of April, I decided to have a barbecue in my back garden. The sun was beating down on the pavement as I sat on the deck chair with my friend Steven. The air was filled with the mouthwatering scent of sizzling sausages and marinated chicken, and the day couldn't have been more perfect. We were chatting, tossing back a couple of cold ones, when Steven dropped a bombshell that would change the course of my business and my life.

My friend Steven was into plumbing and focused on power flush. He was a tall, lanky guy with a business mind as open as the horizon. What I admired most about him was his constant drive for self-improvement and his knack for innovation. He was the kind of person who never settled, always looking for the next big thing. As we sat near the fire, carefully turning the skewers, our conversation naturally drifted towards business, as it often did, and I started to share my business situation with him.

Out of the blue, Steven said, breaking the comfortable silence, "You know, mate, you're busting your hump with electrical work, but you could be making way more cash for way less effort with plumbing (power flush)." Plumbing? I raised an eyebrow, sceptical as ever. I mean, I knew my way around wires and circuits like the back of my hand. The idea of diving into an entirely new trade felt like stepping into uncharted waters.

But Steven had this glint in his eye that said he was onto something big. And heck, who was I to turn down the opportunity for more money and less stress? Additionally, I would never say no to learning. After all, what's the point of working yourself into the ground if there's a smarter way to get ahead?

It wasn't a decision I made lightly, though. After all, I had four months building up my electrical business, and the thought of pivoting to plumbing was both exhilarating and terrifying. The next few weeks were a whirlwind of research, late-night brainstorming sessions, and a growing pile of plumbing manuals. I had a good background in plumbing, but the systems in the UK were different, so it took a bit of studying. I wanted to understand everything—from the intricacies of pipe systems to the latest industry trends. Steven was there every step of the way, nudging me forward, sharing his knowledge, and encouraging me to think bigger.

I even went with him for a few power flushes to learn, and then a week later, I started doing them by myself. A few days after that, we landed a job that would put my newfound interest in plumbing to the test. It was at this massive house on a private island, surrounded by the river Thames. The house was like something out of a dream: an eight-bedroom mansion with a cinema, swimming pool, and God knows what else. The place was owned by a Brazilian lady who was refurbishing it as an investment.

The fact that she could speak my language, Portuguese, made the experience even more enjoyable.

As I walked through the magnificent property with tools in my hand, I couldn't help but feel a sense of awe. Here I was, enjoying the opportunity to contribute to its transformation.

Steven's words echoed in my mind, "You look like a fish that wants to go back to water," he said with a grin. And he was right. I was in my element. The challenge of fitting pipes, solving problems on the fly, and making everything work seamlessly gave me a thrill I hadn't felt in years. We worked on that house multiple times, fine-tuning every detail. When the house was finally completed, it was nothing short of spectacular. A few months later, it was sold, and Steven casually mentioned that the new owner was George Clooney. I couldn't help but chuckle. Knowing that my work was part of something so grand was satisfying, but it didn't change who I was. It just reinforced the belief that I was on the right path.

That experience was the catalyst I needed. I rebranded, changed the company name to EG Power Flush Ltd, and fully immersed myself in the world of pipes and fittings. It wasn't just about making more money; it was about evolving, adapting, and finding joy in the process. As I mentioned, the spark that ignites our journey can sometimes come from the most unexpected places, like a backyard barbecue with a good friend. And that spark? Well, it led me to a world of opportunities I hadn't even imagined.

The shift from electrical work to plumbing wasn't just a career change but a mindset shift. It was about being open to new ideas, trusting in the process, and recognising that growth often requires stepping outside your comfort zone. Sure, it was tough in the beginning, and there were moments when I wondered if I had made a huge mistake. But in the end, the journey from sparks to pipes taught me one invaluable lesson: when you embrace change and take a chance on something new.

Initially, the change looked promising. It felt like I had finally cracked the code to success. I was earning more money than before, landing lucrative contracts left and right. It felt like I was on top of the world, riding the wave of entrepreneurial success that so many people dream of. But as time passed, something began to shift, and the excitement I once felt started to fade. As time went on, I found myself stuck in a routine that was as relentless as it was soul-crushing. My days were a blur of long drives, endless highways, and the monotony of hotel rooms that all started to look the same.

My odometer was spinning out of control, racking up miles like a relentless metronome—30,000 miles per year. In what felt like no time at all, I had driven more than 24,000 miles—that's the equivalent of circling the globe more than once. When you stop and think about it, that's a mind-boggling distance to cover just for work. It was a constant reminder of the hours spent in my van, bouncing from one job to the next.

But I wasn't just letting those hours slip away. During all that time on the road, I made the most of it by listening to Audible, consuming around five books per month on topics like self-development, business and property. It became part of my routine—learning new things, hearing new perspectives, and staying mentally sharp even when the miles kept piling on. Strangely enough, that time in the van became one of my most productive learning environments.

Sometimes, I'd drive to Manchester on a Sunday afternoon to work there on Monday morning. Then, in the afternoon, I'd drive off to Leeds, ready to start on Tuesday, Wednesday in Birmingham, and Thursday in Oxford. By the time Friday or Saturday rolled around, I'd be back home, exhausted and wondering where the week had gone. The cycle repeated up and down the country and week after week, with no end in sight. I'd wake up in a different hotel room every day, the sterile smell of cleaning products becoming all too familiar. I felt like a nomad, constantly moving but never really getting anywhere.

Despite the outward success, something didn't feel right. Sure, the money was great, but a sense of emptiness lingered within me. I'd landed the contracts, secured the deals, and delivered on my promises, but where was the joy? The excitement of being an entrepreneur had faded away, replaced by feelings of monotony and disillusionment. The truth was, in my pursuit of success, I had lost sight of what mattered.

I had forgotten to take care of myself, find moments of happiness, and connect with the things that once brought me joy. Instead, I was caught in this endless loop of work and travel, pushing myself harder and harder, hoping the next big deal would fill the void growing inside me. But it never did.

As the days blurred into one another, I started to notice something else creeping into my life: alcohol. It all began innocently. A drink here and there to relax after a long day, to celebrate a successful deal or a small reward for the long hours and hard work. But slowly, almost imperceptibly, that occasional drink became a regular thing. It became my way of coping with the growing sense of dissatisfaction that I didn't want to acknowledge—a way to escape from the reality that my life was spiralling into something I no longer recognised.

The drinks that started as a way to relax after work turned into a crutch, something to lean on when the emptiness became too much to bear. It was easier to pour myself a drink than to confront the truth that despite all the success, I was deeply unhappy. I didn't see it happening at first, or maybe I didn't want to. I was too busy and too focused on keeping the business running. But deep down, I knew something had to change. I couldn't keep going like this, living a life that looked great on the outside but felt empty inside. The road I was on was leading me nowhere, and it was time to find a new direction.

That realisation didn't come easily, and it didn't come all at once. It crept up on me slowly, in the quiet moments between jobs, in the long drives where I had nothing but my thoughts for company. I started to ask myself the hard questions, "What was I really working for? What was the point of all this if it didn't bring me any happiness?" And most importantly, "what was I going to do about it?"

TAKE OWNERSHIP OF YOUR LIFE

Now, let me ask you a question. Have you ever, at some point in your life, you, too, have found yourself attributing to similar frustration, convinced that the world around you is conspiring against your every effort? We've all been there, right? It's easy to point fingers at these external factors, to believe that our happiness and success are out of our hands, dictated by forces beyond our control. It's a common pattern in life to seek answers externally to our challenges.

But what if I told you that the biggest obstacle isn't out there? What if it's much closer than you think, so close that it's within you?

Let me share a story I heard a few years ago that opened my eyes to this truth. It goes like this:

One day, a man was kneeling on the grass, frantically searching for his house key. Another man approached and, noticing his distress, asked, "What are you doing?" The first man replied, "I'm looking for my house key."

Sympathetic, the second man offered to help. Together, they scoured the grass for 30 minutes, but to no avail. Growing frustrated, the second man asked, "Do you know where you lost the key?" The first man nodded and said, "Yes, inside the house." Perplexed, the second man questioned, "Then why are we searching here?" The first man's response was unexpected yet profound: "Just because here there is light, and inside of the house is dark."

Are you surprised? This story might sound absurd at first, but it conveys a message. We tend to overlook the roots of our problems because it is more comfortable and convenient where we feel in control, even if it's not where the problem actually lies. Think about it. How often do we do the same thing? We avoid the shadows, the uncomfortable truths, and the deeper introspection because it's easier to look where things are already apparent. However, the reality is that many of our difficulties originate from inside, our fears, uncertainties and self-imposed limitations. In a word, it's our mindset.

Similar to the man searching for his lost key in the light, we often avoid dealing with the darkness and complexities of our minds. Yet, the only way to truly find what we're looking for is to turn inward, face the darkness, and shine a light on those hidden corners of ourselves. By doing so, we not only find the solutions we seek but also empower ourselves to overcome challenges and create real, lasting change in our lives.

One of the best and most transformative decisions I've ever made was to take full responsibility for my life. It's a shift in perspective from feeling and seeing myself as a victim of circumstances to empowered architects of my own reality. I have a role in shaping every experience I encounter.

Once you adopt this mindset, something incredible will happen. You will realise that your thoughts, beliefs and actions directly influence the outcomes you experience. It's not about blaming yourself for every setback or failure. Instead, it's about acknowledging your role in crafting your path. As the saying goes,

> “Life doesn't happen to you; it happens for you.”

At the core of this concept lies the power of perspective. What we believe and focus on becomes our reality. If you fixate on negativity and limitations, that's exactly what you'll attract into your life. But if you choose to cultivate a dynamic mindset, you open yourself up to a world of possibilities and potential.

Think of it this way: Your perspective acts as the operating system for your mind. The information you consistently input moulds your behaviours, attitudes, and, ultimately, your life. This is why you must be significantly vigilant about the thoughts you entertain and the influences you allow into your life every day.

As you can see, taking ownership of your life means taking responsibility for the narrative you tell yourself. It's about deciding that you have the power to change, grow, and create the life you want, regardless of what's happening around you. It's about realising that the key to your happiness and success isn't lost outside in the grass—it's right inside you, waiting to be found.

So, how do you start this journey of ownership?

Begin by acknowledging the areas of your life where you've been searching in the wrong places. Where have you been looking for external solutions to internal problems? Where have you been avoiding the darkness within in favour of the comfort of the light? Once you identify these areas, take a deep breath and be willing to step into the shadows. It might be uncomfortable at first, but it's in this discomfort that real growth happens.

So, remember, the most important work you can do is the work within. As you take ownership of your thoughts, beliefs, and actions, you'll see that you are not at the mercy of life. You are the creator of it. And with that realisation comes an incredible sense of freedom and power.

> “ Take 100% responsibility for your life! ”

REDEFINING SUCCESS

Throughout my life, I've always had a burning desire to shake things up and carve out my path. Despite trying out jobs and exploring ideas, I often needed clarification about my true aspirations. It was like I was wandering through life without a clear destination, driven by this vague sense that there was something more, something I was meant to do, but I just couldn't put my finger on it. It was like grappling with a puzzle that remained unsolved.

Then, out of nowhere, a memory from my youth that I mentioned in Chapter 1 resurfaced. Little did I know that within my little mind, I had already set a goal to shape my life in ways. When I was six, I offhandedly mentioned, "I'll retire at 42". It was a fleeting comment, a fanciful idea stemming from youthful innocence.

Reflecting on it now, I realised it wasn't just a casual comment. As time passed and I journeyed through life's twists and turns, that insignificant statement gained meaning, a guiding beacon lighting the way ahead.

It showed me a hidden feeling deep down, a feeling that guided me without me knowing. Even though I didn't understand it back then, it made me think about what I wanted in life. As I looked within myself, I learned that real change comes from understanding ourselves, not just changing what's around us.

As I matured, my perspective evolved. When I turned thirty, something clicked in my mind. I started to see things differently, especially when I thought about my dad. I started grasping the intricacies of adulthood and the responsibilities that come with it. Early retirement at 42 became a symbol of financial independence and self-rule. However, the core of my childhood aspiration stayed consistent.

It wasn't about reaching an age or retiring but taking charge of my life. I didn't want to work out of necessity. I wanted to work out of choice.

I remembered how hard he worked when he was my age and all the sacrifices he made to secure a future for us. I remember vividly when we relocated from Venezuela to Madeira when I was six years old. The big move signified a turning point for us, filled with hope and aspirations for a brighter tomorrow. Back then, I viewed my dad as elderly in his forties, but now I truly appreciate his strength and resilience. Despite the belief that starting anew in your forties may be too late, my dad exemplified that it's never too late to embark on new endeavours.

His unwavering determination and perseverance during times left a lasting impact on me. Reflecting on everything he sacrificed for our family fills me with gratitude and pride. His teachings on the value of work and perseverance have left a mark on me.

Reflecting on everything he sacrificed for our family fills me with a deep sense of gratitude and pride. His example taught me the true meaning of hard work and the value of perseverance. It also showed me that success isn't about reaching a certain milestone by a certain age—it's about the journey, the lessons learned along the way, and the impact we have on those we love.

As I navigated through my own struggles, my dad's example became a beacon of hope. It reminded me that it's okay to change course, redefine what success means, and focus on what truly matters. My dad didn't let age or circumstances hold him back; he kept pushing forward, driven by a sense of purpose and a desire to create a better life for us.

That's when I started to see the bigger picture. I realised that the fulfilment I was searching for would come from something other than external achievements or material possessions. It would come from aligning my life with my true values, cultivating meaningful relationships, and finding a purpose beyond just making money.

This shift in perspective was liberating. It allowed me to let go of the relentless pursuit of external validation and focus on what really matters. Taking ownership of my life wasn't just about making more money or achieving more success—it was about redefining what success meant to me. I didn't grasp the concept of a dynamic mindset in the past. It never occurred to me that the issue might not lie with the world but within myself.

However, as I delved deeper into understanding it, things started to click for me. I began noticing some changes in my life, which were developments. Yet progress wasn't happening as swiftly as I had hoped. Initially, I believed I could rectify everything instantaneously. That turned out to be a misconception. It required time and patience to bring about transformations.

At times, engaging in a job can feel like being trapped in a cycle of labour without reaping the rewards. However, my aspiration is not to labour within my business; instead, I aspire to work on its growth—I aim to steer its direction, motivate others and strive for achievement. Work isn't about gain; it also pertains to finding joy and maintaining good health.

Authentic wealth lies in experiences, connections with others and the pleasure of existence. While many view a job merely as a means of survival, I firmly believe there's more depth to it than meets the eye. It's about discovering purpose and embracing life wholeheartedly.

Therefore, as I progress through life's journey, I strive for more than compensation. My goal is to effect change and lead a fulfilling life by cherishing every moment.

Following my interests and living on my terms became the driving motivation behind my dreams.

Think of mindset as a journey; it's not something you can turn on or off at will. It's similar to climbing a ladder, moving from one rung to the next. You can't skip any rungs; you must climb them step by step.

So, as you navigate your journey, I encourage you to take a step back and ask yourself:

What does success really mean to you?
Are you chasing after something that's truly meaningful, or are you caught up in the pursuit of external validation?
Are you living in alignment with your values, or are you compromising your happiness for the sake of others' expectations?

SETTING GOALS

As I sit here, reflecting on the journey that led to the creation of this book, I'm struck by how much has changed since I first recognised the power of setting goals. It's funny, isn't it? We often think that goals are just tasks on a to-do list, items to be checked off as we move through life. But the truth is, they're so much more than that. Goals are the compass that guides us. They're the bridge between where we are and where we want to be. Goals are a vital part of my life now.

Looking back, I realise that it wasn't just about setting goals but about the 'emotion' attached to my goals.

I didn't fully grasp it as a child, but I felt it: a longing for something more, a desire for a richer, more satisfying existence. That feeling, that deep emotional connection to my dreams, was what truly fuelled my ambition. It wasn't just about achieving something but about fulfilling a need deep within me. And that's the key: our goals must resonate with us deeply and emotionally. They need to mean something more than just a line on a piece of paper.

That's why, even now, that childhood vision remains ever-present in my thoughts. It's a constant reminder of why I strive and push forward with conviction and purpose. It's why I've learned to pursue my passions with unwavering dedication. Because I know now that goals are not just about reaching a destination; they're about the journey, the growth, and the transformation that happens along the way.

Take this book, for example. Yes, the very book you're holding in your hands right now. It's more than just words on paper; it's the realisation of a dream. You see, writing a book had been on my list of goals for at least five years, one of those dreams that felt distant yet always present. Although it was like a secondary goal, it was one of those dreams I held close to my heart. It was a goal that lingered at the back of my mind, waiting for the right moment to come to life.

And then, life happened, as it always does. A few months ago, I attended an event; little did I know that it was about to change everything.

I was just going through the motions, mingling with the crowd, when I met someone who would play a pivotal role in this journey: my publisher. It was one of those moments that felt like fate, like the universe was giving me a nudge, whispering, "Here's your chance. I have to act now!"

This serendipitous encounter sparked something in me, a fire, a determination that had been simmering for years but now roared to life. Suddenly, the distant dream of writing a book felt within reach. It was as if the universe had handed me the keys to success. And I knew, in that moment, that I couldn't let the opportunity slip away. So, what did I do next?

I took action, plain and simple!

I booked a meeting with my publisher, shared my ideas, and poured my heart into this project. And now, here we are. You're reading the result of that effort, the manifestation of a dream that was once just a whisper in my heart.

It's funny how life works, isn't it? How can the things we dream of and our goals come to life when we least expect them?

But that's the beauty of it. The universe is always listening, always ready to give us a nudge in the right direction. We have to be ready to act when the opportunity presents itself.

THE 90/10 RULE OF MINDSET

Success is fuelled by a mindset, they say. Just like I mentioned about my own experience, when it comes to reaching our goals, it's often mentioned that 90% of the challenge lies in our mindset while the remaining 10% is about taking action. Think of it this way: our mindset serves as the compass that directs us on our journey. Like using GPS navigation, if we set the wrong destination, we'll end up far from where we intended to go. The same principle applies to our goals. Without the right mindset, we won't achieve what we set out to achieve.

So, how do we ensure we have the mindset? It all starts with clarity. We must understand where we want to go and what we aim to accomplish. Like entering the address into a GPS, having a clear destination in our mind is crucial.

However, here's the thing: knowing our destination is only part of the equation. We also need to remind ourselves of our goals. As I explained earlier, it's similar to tending to a plant; if we neglect it, it will wither away. The same applies to our goals; they will materialise if we nurture them with our thoughts and actions. Another way of seeing it is our subconscious mind works like the driver of a car. If we provide it with directions, aka, our goals and dreams, it will find a way to guide us there. However, if we keep changing our destination or fail to give it the right instructions, it will default to whatever else's occupying our thoughts.

This is why some people face challenges in reaching their objectives. They begin with intentions but then become distracted or lose focus, leading them astray before they realise it. The encouraging news is that it's never too late to make corrections. By reminding yourself of your goals and taking steps towards them each day, you can steer yourself back to the life you aspire for.

So, as we come to the end of this chapter, I want you to remember this: Your goals are more than just dreams. They're a roadmap to your future, a blueprint for the life you want to create. And when you tie them to something more profound, an emotion, a passion, a longing, they become achievable.

Don't just set goals. Feel them. Live them. Let them guide you, fuel you, and push you toward the life you're meant to live. Because when you do, you'll find that the universe is on your side, ready to help you turn those dreams into reality.

THE FINAL LEAP

As we reach the end of this journey, I want to reflect on everything we've covered and my journey to an uncertain, terrifying plunge into the unknown. And as we've navigated the ups and downs, the struggles and breakthroughs, one truth has become crystal clear: success isn't about luck or talent alone; it's about consistency, belief, and the willingness to take action, even when the path ahead is unclear.

You see, goals serve as the blueprint for your dreams, guiding you towards your desired destinations. However, having a blueprint isn't enough. You need to build the structure, brick by brick, day by day. It's not just about setting goals; it's about making them a part of who you are. When we establish a goal, we aren't merely creating a wish list but embedding and imprinting it on our subconscious mind.

For instance, each morning, the first thing you must do is remind yourself of your goals. It's like playing a movie in your mind where you're the main character, living out the life you've always imagined. This practice is powerful because it helps you internalise your goals, turning them into a core part of your mindset.

Your mindset is like the background software of your life. It runs quietly in the background, influencing every thought, decision, and action you take. By fuelling it with affirmations like "I'm healthy, I'm happy, I'm prosperous," its transformative power begins to take effect. Your subconscious registers these messages, and they start to align with your behaviour. But let's be honest: this doesn't happen overnight. Consistency is key in this practice.

I will cover more about affirmation in Chapter 6, but for now, you must keep repeating those affirmations every day until they sink in, and you truly believe them with all your heart.

As I mentioned, it's not just about saying them; it's about feeling and living by them. This is where positive affirmations can be so helpful. They act as boosts for your aspirations. Linking them to your goals makes them more robust and tangible. Saying them aloud in the present sentences breathes life into them, infusing them with energy.

Now, here's the key ingredient: emotion. Remember I mentioned earlier that emotion propels your ambitions forward? The more you feel the excitement, joy, and satisfaction of achieving your goals, the more driven you become.

So, when you recite your affirmations, don't just go through the motions. Feel them. Experience the joy of being healthy, the thrill of happiness, the richness of prosperity. Let those emotions wash over you and drive you forward, even when motivation wanes. Because, let's face it, motivation is fickle. It's easy to start strong and lose steam when the results take time.

But remember, motivation is simply "motive" plus "action." You already have the motives, which are your goals and aspirations. All that's left is to take action. What better catalyst for action than emotion?

And action, my friend, is where the magic happens. It's like going to the gym. You don't see the results after the first day or even the first week.

But if you keep showing up and putting in the work day after day, you'll eventually start to see the changes. The same is true for your goals. If you do a little bit every day, you'll begin to see your dreams getting closer and closer until, one day, you'll realise you've achieved them.

As we close this chapter, I want to leave you with this: Your journey doesn't end here. A leap into the unknown is just the beginning. It's the first step on a path that will challenge, test, and ultimately transform you. There will be days when the road is hard, progress feels slow, and doubts creep in.

But remember this: every small step and tiny action brings you closer to your goal.

Keep believing in yourself, visualising your dreams, and taking action. Embrace the unknown because it's in those uncertain moments that you'll find your true strength.

You've already taken the first leap; it's time to keep moving forward with purpose, passion, and the unwavering belief that you have everything it takes to succeed.

If you risk nothing, then you risk everything.

Rob Moore

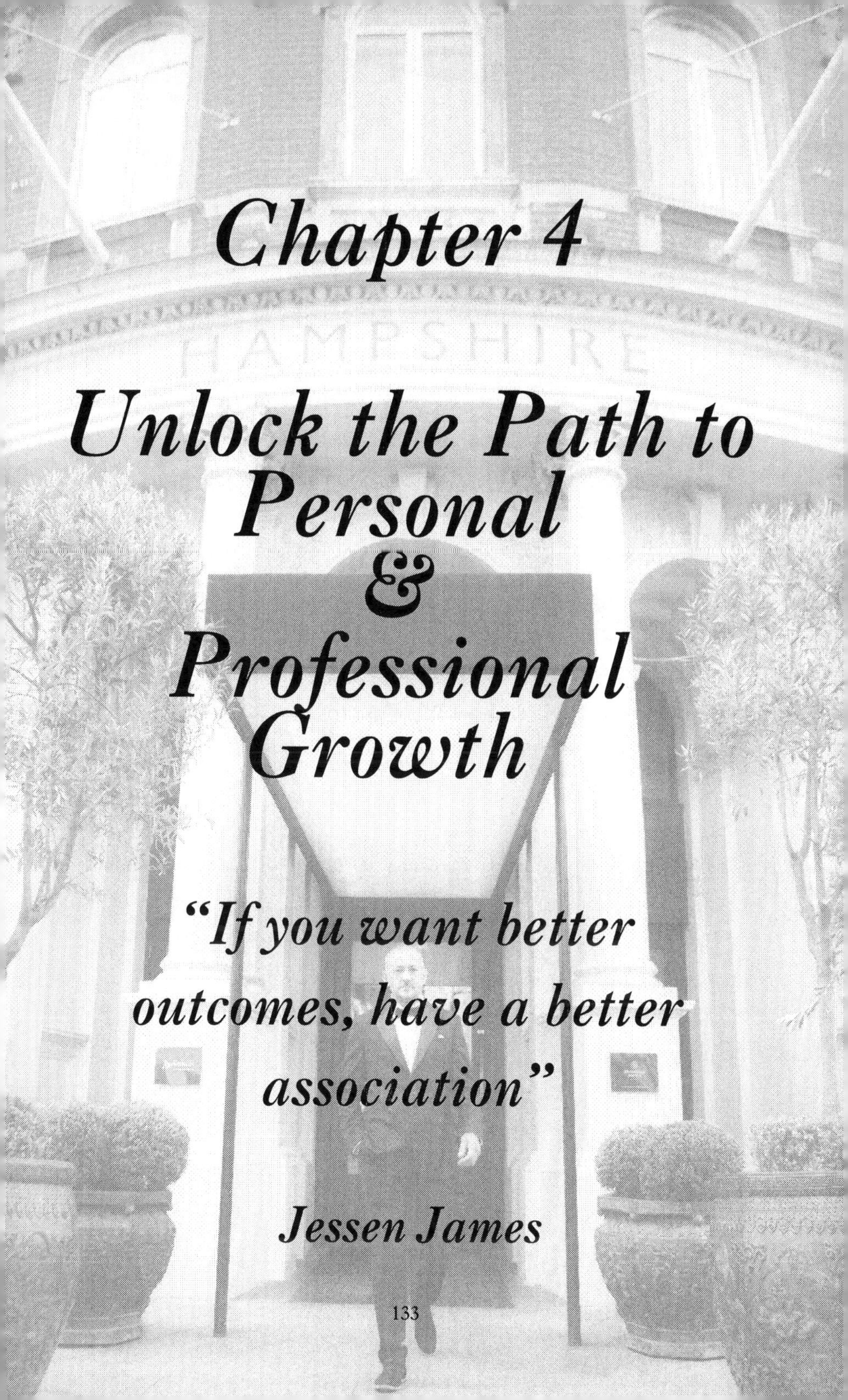

Chapter 4

Unlock the Path to Personal & Professional Growth

"If you want better outcomes, have a better association"

Jessen James

UNLOCK THE PATH TO PERSONAL & PROFESSIONAL GROWTH

In the previous chapter, we delved into the thrilling yet the courage of taking a leap into the unknown, in my case, my entrepreneurship journey. This leap is full of fear and doubt, but it is a crucial step for every entrepreneur because the unknown, though terrifying, is where actual growth begins.

It is the moment when you break free from the comfort of the known and explore unexplored horizons, leading to self-discovery and empowerment. It's where you challenge your limits, push past your fears, and discover new potentials within yourself.

Like any great adventure, navigating through the unknown requires more than courage; it demands guidance, wisdom, and a clear sense of direction. It's in these moments that mentorship makes all the difference.

That's why, in this chapter, I delve into the importance of mentorship events and networking. These serve as tools for your personal and professional development.

Nonetheless, there's an overlooked element: balance.

MASTERY WITH MENTORSHIP

Ralph Waldo Emerson once said,

> Success is not a destination; it's a journey.

That journey becomes all the more fulfilling when you have the right guide by your side. I realised this early in my entrepreneurial journey. I needed guidance, big time! I needed someone experienced by my side. Someone who had walked the path before and someone who could help me find my way. A mentor was what I needed. So, amid all the chaos of entrepreneurship, I made a decision that changed everything. I decided to seek a mentor who could provide insights, steer me clear of pitfalls and help me unlock my full potential.

Let me tell you, it was a decision I had to make because, at first, the idea seemed overwhelming. I had questions swirling in my mind like a swarm of bees. Who would be the right mentor for me? What qualities should I seek in a mentor? How could I approach them without coming off as inexperienced? It felt like trying to solve a Rubik's Cube blindfolded – puzzling, frustrating and kind of scary. However, deep down, I understood that finding a mentor was crucial for unlocking my entrepreneurial potential.

So, filled with determination and a plethora of queries, I embarked on a journey in search of mentorship that would forever alter the course of my entrepreneurship journey.

Alright, buckle up because we're delving into the year that truly made an impact. In March 2013, three months into my entrepreneurial endeavour, I enrolled in a mastermind course led by the legendary Jack Canfield. Yeah, you heard me right, THE Jack Canfield – the guy behind the "Chicken Soup for the Soul" series, the movie "The Secret" and a transformative figure in personal development. Now, I'm not going to lie. I was filled with anticipation and mixed emotions – excitement and nervousness. However, little did I know that this decision would start a journey that would reshape my world in ways I could never have imagined.

Over a year, I actively participated in this program through weekly calls for six months that later transitioned to monthly sessions. Imagine being part of a community dedicated to growth, spending a year immersed in knowledge, skill enhancement, and connection-building. It felt like being part of a community dedicated to growth and achievement. The wisdom I gained, the strategies I learned, and the connections I built with members of this group led to changes I never imagined were possible.

My business started booming. That was just the beginning. The actual transformation I experienced happened deep within me, touching every aspect of my being. Mentally, emotionally and spiritually, I evolved into a version of myself that I never imagined possible. This new version of me was equipped and ready to take on any challenge that life could throw my way.

A significant part of this evolution was fuelled by studying Jack Canfield's book, The Success Principles. This book, packed with 64 powerful principles for achieving success, became my roadmap to personal and professional growth. I can't recommend it enough—if you're serious about changing your life, this book is a must-read.

So, why am I sharing all this with you? Because I want you to understand that real, lasting change is achievable for anyone willing to take the crucial first step. Change isn't just possible; it's inevitable when you're committed to it. With the right guidance and encouragement, you can accomplish anything you set your mind to.

Under Jack Canfield's mentorship, I encountered a transformation that went far beyond business strategies or professional skills. It was a transformation of the heart and mind that reshaped my entire outlook on life. This journey taught me that with the right tools, mindset, and mentor, you can unlock levels of success and fulfilment that you never thought possible.

During a mastermind session with Jack Canfield, I shared with him what my friend Steven suggested in Chapter 3 about going into plumbing, and he and his team helped me understand the transition and guided me through the process. I didn't just enhance my business; I rebranded it, focused my efforts and achieved levels of success that once seemed unattainable.

I remember telling Jack that I wanted to earn at least £2000 per month, and a few months later, I started making in a week. But this journey wasn't about achieving my objectives but about evolving into a better version of myself, personally and professionally.

Just like every journey has its end, so did this phase of growth and development for me eventually reached its conclusion. As my annual business mentorship program wrapped up, I took some time to reflect on the profound growth I had experienced. It was a bittersweet moment. While I was proud of how far I had come, I also felt a mix of nervousness and excitement about what lay ahead. Despite all the progress I had made over the years, I soon found myself facing yet another challenging moment in my life.

You see, even after all that growth, I found myself at a crossroads where complacency threatened to stall my growth. It's funny how life works sometimes; when you think you've figured it all out, it throws you a curveball. Progress, which had once seemed like a natural flow, now felt almost impossible to achieve again.

Trapped in the monotony of routine, I started to struggle with a feeling of inertia. Days blended into weeks and weeks into months as I worked tirelessly, pushing myself to exhaustion. As mentioned in Chapter 3, my professional duties required unwavering dedication, and I found myself constantly on the move, travelling miles each year for work throughout England and Wales.

While I was grateful for the opportunities that came with my job, the relentless travel schedule left little room for anything else. As the miles added up, so did the feeling of being stretched too thin. The time I spent on the road was time away from my family, from rest, and from simply being present in my own life.

It's a tough place to be, where you're doing everything right on the surface, but internally, you're struggling to keep it all together. The irony is that the drive that had fuelled my success now threatened to burn me out. I knew I needed to find a way to regain balance.

I needed to reconnect with the deeper purpose that had guided me through my journey of transformation in the first place.

STEP INTO ACTIONS

In 2014, I made a fundamental decision to diversify my investments and step out of my comfort zone by exploring property investment. With a mix of excitement and determination, I signed up for a property course in London, eager to soak up knowledge and tap into networking opportunities. I was enthusiastic and ready to dive into deals and start my property portfolio. However, despite all the excitement, I didn't pursue any deals as planned. The challenges of securing investors and the lack of action on my part held me back.

Looking back, I realised how important it is to take action, a concept I also learnt from The Success Principles book I mentioned earlier. An entire chapter is dedicated to taking 100% responsibility for your life. But somehow, I kept finding myself too busy or making excuses, preventing me from taking the necessary steps. I used to tell myself, "I don't know anyone with money to invest," and other similar reasons for my inaction. I failed to see that I could have tapped into my existing network—friends and family, or even reached out through community events or networking opportunities to find potential investors.

But with no mentor to guide me, I ended up giving up. At the time, it felt like I was stuck, unsure of the following steps or how to navigate the obstacles I was facing. Looking back, I realise how valuable it would have been to have someone in my corner, someone with experience who could help me see the bigger picture and push me in the right direction.

Over the years, I embarked on a seven-hour drive to Scotland for another property seminar. Now, you won't believe what unfolded during the journey!

Despite the long drive and the anticipation, the result was the same as before. I learned a lot, made great connections and networked with like-minded individuals. I gained so much insight and building relationships, but progress seemed hard to come by.

On top of that, I found juggling my business responsibilities while exploring opportunities quite challenging. Diversifying seemed like a smart move at the time, but dealing with investors and property transactions proved more difficult than I anticipated. Even though the path ahead was unclear and obstacles continued to arise, I remained committed to facing these challenges with resolve and unwavering dedication. I understood it was part of the journey and was determined to see it through.

You see, the journey of entrepreneurship is far from a straight line. It's a rollercoaster of successes and setbacks. Despite encountering obstacles, every challenge I faced added to my resilience and inner strength. Looking back, I realise that the lessons I learned were not just about business; they were about life. On this journey, I recall the teachings I absorbed from Jack Canfield,

> Success is not merely about achieving goals; it's about embracing the journey itself, with all its twists, turns, and moments of introspection, serving as a building block for my growth.

The thing is, you may attend events, acquire new knowledge, and connect with influential individuals, but if you fail to act on your learnings and the relationships you've built, it all becomes futile.

Let me exemplify this using a scenario. Do you recall Nokia? Back in 2004, Nokia reigned supreme in the mobile phone sector. I was a user of their phones. However, they suddenly vanished. Why? Due to their lack of innovation. As the era of smartphones emerged, Nokia presumed that their loyal customer base wouldn't embrace new technologies. They relied on their past triumphs and neglected to adapt to the evolving market landscape. Yet their customers wanted something new. Nokia's resistance to change led to its downfall. This highlights the significance of taking action, adapting to change, and being innovative.

Complacency can result in stagnation, whether in business endeavours or personal pursuits. So, you must continue progressing, learning, and adjusting. Merely knowing what needs to be done isn't sufficient; you must also take massive action and always be innovative.

By taking steps, you'll notice the universe reciprocating positively, and doors of opportunity will open, leading to success. The crucial thing is to keep progressing one step after another and keep a dynamic mindset. It's about moving forward, staying adaptable, open to learning, and ready to adjust your approach when needed.

A dynamic mindset allows you to pivot when challenges arise and see possibilities where others might only see roadblocks. That's how you continue to grow, even when the path can be challenging.

THE RESET

Do you remember the early days of 2020, when the whole world suddenly hit the pause button? The pandemic had us all locked up in our homes with more time on our hands than we knew what to do with. It was a strange, unsettling time for everyone, and I was no exception. But while most people were navigating the madness from their living rooms, I found myself in a place I least expected: stuck in a hospital bed for a solid two weeks.

It all started one morning when I noticed something odd with my vision. I was driving and suddenly saw what looked like a cloud hovering in the corner of my left eye. It was weird and a little unsettling, so I did what most people would: I called my GP. They didn't mince words. They told me to head straight to the main hospital because it involved my vision, and it sounded serious. Oh, and they made it clear I shouldn't drive myself there. So, I called my brother, and he rushed over to take me.

After hours of tests, the doctors broke the news that they were going to keep me overnight. My blood pressure had skyrocketed to a dangerous 232/108, and a vein had ruptured in my left eye, leaving me unable to focus properly on it. To be honest, I had no idea it was that bad until they explained how serious it was. I went out to tell my brother I'd be staying the night, but as soon as I stepped outside, I was hit by this blinding daylight.

My eyes were super sensitive because of the drops they used during the tests, so I couldn't see a thing. I reached for my phone to call my brother but couldn't even read the screen. At that moment, I was so frustrated.

My vision was a blur, and I felt so helpless. I decided to go to the last call and hope for the best. If it weren't my brother, maybe it would be someone who knew him and could help me reach him. Thankfully, I managed to call my brother, and I could hear his phone ringing beside me.

He answered, surprised, "Why are you calling me? I am right here!" I was so shocked and frustrated because I could not see. I broke down in tears and told him, "I can't see anything, and you might as well go home because I'm staying here for the night."

That night turned into two weeks; let me tell you, those two weeks felt like an eternity. Hospitals have never been my favourite place, and this stay was particularly rough. I spent the first four nights in the ICU, hooked up to machines that monitored my heart rate, blood pressure, and other things. This stay was particularly memorable, but it was not a nice one! Every time I'd start to drift off to sleep, the blood pressure cuff would kick into action with that terrifying noise and horrible squeezing sensation, waking me up.

It felt like a never-ending nightmare.

On top of that, there was the daily COVID test, a miserable routine, and I wasn't exactly thrilled with the hospital food either. All I wanted was to get out of there and return to my life, home, and bed. I even longed to return to work. But instead, I was stuck, counting down the days, wondering when I'd finally be able to leave. It was one of the most frustrating experiences of my life, and I wouldn't wish it on anyone. When I finally left the hospital, I was still weak but determined.

And what was my next move? Well, let me save you from guessing!

I made a decision that seemed reasonable at the time: I chose to jump straight into another property course. It might have seemed like an odd choice to others, considering everything I had just been through, but it felt like the natural next step for me. This time, the course was two full days on Zoom, so there was no need to leave home or step out. It was a way to keep moving forward while still managing my situation.

To understand why, let's go back seven years. That's when my interest in property investment began. Eager and ambitious, I entered the realm of property with optimism. I signed up for my first course guided by a mentor who had everything figured out. They had the success story, the knowledge, and the blueprint that I was sure would lead me to my success.

I threw myself into the learning process, absorbing every piece of information like a sponge and putting in the effort to make it work. But as often happens in life, things don't go according to plan. Yes, again!

Despite my best efforts, success remained elusive. I hit roadblocks I hadn't anticipated, encountering confusion and disappointment at almost every turn. The world of property investment, which had seemed so promising, was suddenly filled with complexities I wasn't prepared for.

That's the thing about life: it's full of twists and turns, and sometimes it feels like you're moving backwards instead of forward. There were moments when I seriously questioned whether I was on the right path and whether all this effort was worth it. But even in those moments of doubt, I knew deep down that the journey itself was part of the experience.

The setbacks, frustrations, and unexpected detours were all part of the story, even if they weren't the chapters I had planned on writing.

So here I was again, years later, feeling like I was back at square one. At least, that's how it seemed to me. I still had little to show after learning from property mentors and investing time and energy into various courses. The excitement I once felt for property investment had faded, replaced by a growing sense of frustration and self-doubt. I started questioning whether all those courses were worth it.

But then something shifted, something that changed everything.

In 2019, I bought my home. I decided to apply what I learned from those property courses and refurbished the house. Two years later, I refinanced, increasing the equity in the property. This move not only boosted the value of the house but also made my mortgage payments much more affordable. It was the first actual proof that the knowledge I had gained could pay off. It reignited my belief that I wasn't back at square one after all—those courses had laid the groundwork for a solid strategy, and now I was finally seeing the results.

I've always found solace in the night sky. Sometimes, I sit outside watching the stars, and I love how it always helps me think deeply and see things more clearly. One of those nights was exceptional. As I stared up at the stars, lost in thought, I had a realisation that hit me like a bolt of lightning.

The problem wasn't with the mentors I had relied on or the external circumstances that seemed to conspire against me. The issue was within me, within my mindset. I had spent so long blaming external factors for my lack of progress, convincing myself that I would have succeeded if only this or that had been different.

I realised that I hadn't taken full responsibility for my journey.

I had been waiting for someone else to guide me, to show me the way, instead of taking charge and carving out my path. With a heavy heart, I accepted that my current methods weren't yielding results. My efforts, while genuine, were falling short. The signs could no longer be ignored. It was time for a reset—a fresh start.

I had to change my approach to life, not just property investment. I had to stop making excuses and blaming others. I had to make the necessary changes, shift my mindset, and start again with renewed focus and determination.

Any journey in life, whether personal, professional or financial, doesn't have to follow a straight line, and our mindset determines whether those twists and turns derail us or help us grow. It's easy to get stuck in a fixed mindset, where every failure feels like a dead end, every setback like a personal flaw. That's where I had been for too long, thinking I wasn't cut out for success because things didn't work out as planned. But life doesn't work that way.

This time, I was going to be the one in control of my journey, with or without a mentor by my side. It was time to reset, to take a deep breath, and to begin again—this time with the understanding that the power to succeed was in my hands all along. But more than that, I was ready to embrace a dynamic mindset that allowed growth, change, and adaptation.

SURROUND YOURSELF WITH SUCCESS

Now that you understand the importance of having a mentor, let's discuss the importance of the company we keep because the people we surround ourselves with can significantly influence our mindset and, ultimately, our achievements. You've likely heard the phrase,

> "You're the average of the five people spend the most time with."

And there is truth in that statement. This idea hinges on mirroring, where our minds are trained to reflect the behaviours and attitudes of those around us. Have you ever noticed how if someone near you yawns, you often start to yawn, too? That's a simple example of how our brains mimic others' actions without us even realising it. This mirroring goes beyond physical actions. It also extends to our thoughts and behaviours.

Now, think about it: if we can easily mirror something like yawning, we also mirror more significant aspects of those around us. Imagine your five closest friends are all very successful in business. By spending time with them, you will naturally start to adopt their habits, mindset, and approaches to business.

You begin to absorb their knowledge and attitudes without even trying, leading to your success.

Think of a time when you were in the company of people who motivated, supported, and encouraged you, it ignited a spark within you to pursue your aspirations, right? Conversely, being consistently surrounded by negativity, scepticism, and contentment may hinder you from realising your true potential. That's why it's essential to be mindful of who you include in your inner circle.

Each time you engage with someone, it's vital to ask yourself whether this relationship or conversation will contribute positively to your life or not.

This practice will compel you to assess how your connections impact your mindset and goals. The more you employ this question, the instinctively you will steer clear of people who do not align with your best interests. Honestly, there are times when you might outgrow friendships as you go through a mindset shift on your journey towards growth and success. Instead of perceiving it as something negative, take it as a blessing that no one will drag you down.

The beauty lies in the fact that as you change your mindset and progress towards your objectives, you often motivate those in your circle to do the same. I've personally witnessed this phenomenon. I observed changes in my friendships when I started focusing on my goals and connecting with friends who shared my aspirations and principles. Some naturally drifted apart while others stepped up and transformed themselves, too.

You see, you have the capacity to influence and inspire those around you by staying true to yourself and your goals. Therefore, choosing your circle and surrounding yourself with individuals who uplift you is essential. By doing so, there is no limit to what you can accomplish. There is a known quote attributed to Jim Rohn that says,

> Show me your friends, and I'll show you your future.

As mentioned earlier, these words ring true as the individuals we choose to associate significantly shape our perspectives and guide our future. To shift our mindset and life trajectory, we might face choices regarding who we allow into our circle. Making decisions that benefit us without excluding others is crucial.

Adjusting to change can be challenging, especially when it means moving on from relationships that no longer add value to our lives. However, it's a part of growth and finding fulfilment. The silver lining is that we open ourselves up to opportunities by welcoming like-minded individuals into our lives.

So, it is vital that you evaluate your inner circle carefully. Are the people around you encouraging your goals and dreams? If not, perhaps it's time for some adjustments. The company we keep influences our path in life, so choose wisely.

NETWORKING GOLDMINE

Fast forward a few years to 2022, I decided it was time to step up my game and signed up for a business mastermind group to boost my business. Naturally, I started sharing my intentions and experiences with my sister, and she, in turn, passed them along to my mum. With her caring and practical nature, my mum always emphasised the importance of hard work and commitment. She urged me to focus on building a secure future, encouraging me to prioritise a stable career over attending events or diving too deeply into personal development.

Her advice, of course, came from a place of love and concern for my well-being, shaped by her experiences and what she believed would help me succeed. She wasn't trying to discourage me but wanted to protect me from uncertainty. And this is where I realised something significant: sometimes, the people closest to us, though they mean well, might not fully understand the path we choose. It's not out of ill intent—they see the world differently based on their experiences.

While I deeply respected her perspective, there was something inside me that wouldn't fade. I had this drive, a desire to explore beyond the traditional path, to create a life that was uniquely my own. It wasn't just about working hard; it was about aligning my work with my passions, my dreams, and what truly resonated with me.

Personal development and networking are often misunderstood by people who haven't experienced them firsthand. They might seem unnecessary or frivolous to outsiders, but in reality, these are the gold mines for growth, learning, and creating meaningful connections that push you forward in life.

Little did I know, this decision to invest in myself was about to unlock a whole new world for me. As part of the program, I found myself in a 12-month mastermind group called The Millionaire Master Mind, run by Joseph Valente. This wasn't just about business strategies; it was about surrounding myself with like-minded individuals who understood what I was trying to do, even if those closest to me didn't. This network and community became a source of invaluable knowledge, motivation, and opportunity. Like Jessen James also says,

> "Your circle impacts your success."

The mastermind group was unique, unlike anything you've ever encountered! Just imagine this: every month, we gathered in the heart of London, trust me, not in the usual dull meeting spaces. We switched things up by exploring twelve locations, each more captivating than the last. We started at Sunborn Yacht Hotel and finished at The Gherkin. Then, we indulged in luxury hotels that treated us like royalty. And that's not all. We even ascended to the top of the Shard, mingling with the clouds as we exchanged ideas.

At every mastermind session, they brought in two speakers who were true experts in their fields, from business acumen to personal growth.

I've had the chance to connect with over 30 high-net-worth individuals and interacted with over 50 like-minded individuals who were all striving to grow their businesses. It's a different world there, but let me share something with you. I've come across some valuable opportunities. Initially, I navigated through these gatherings, engaging in conversations, exchanging business cards, and hoping for the best. But guess what?

Networking goes beyond gathering contacts; it's about fostering connections. Consider this. Every person you meet at the mastermind sessions could unveil doors to possibilities. Those mentors? They're like hidden gems in a sea of familiar faces. Some of them began as names on a list. Now? They feel like part of my inner circle, almost like family. It's incredible how a casual chat over coffee or a brief interaction at an event can lead to great opportunities. I consider myself blessed that I crossed paths with some truly remarkable individuals, people who not only inspired me but also changed the course of my life.

Being part of the mentorship program was an incredible opportunity, mainly because it included a 1:1 session with the amazing Mike Grene. Mike is known not only as the former "Secret Millionaire" but also for leading Morrisons' £20 million takeover.

He's a highly experienced, wise, and approachable person. Every month, I would drive to Peterborough for a mentoring session with him, and it was worth every mile.

These meetings had a profound impact on both me and my business. Mike's wealth of knowledge and deep understanding of business are unparalleled. I remember going in, convinced I had some genuinely complex problems that would challenge even him. But every single time, without fail, he had the answer right at his fingertips, almost as if he knew exactly what I was going to ask. His insights were not just helpful but transformative.

I've learned so much from Mike and continue to do so whenever I have the chance to meet him. His guidance has shaped the way I approach challenges and navigate the complexities of business. It's been a privilege to be mentored by someone with such a remarkable track record and a genuine desire to help others succeed.

Through these events, I also had the chance to meet Alfie Best, known by many as the 'Gypsy Billionaire.' He's a self-made entrepreneur who built an empire that includes 100 residential parks. His story is the epitome of resilience and determination, and meeting him left a lasting impression on me. In fact, after that first meeting, I had the pleasure of crossing paths with him two more times in 2023 and once more in 2024. I always walked away feeling inspired by his wisdom and deep business knowledge.

Then, there was Matt Fiddes, another remarkable figure I had the privilege to meet. Matt is best known as Michael Jackson's former bodyguard, but his accomplishments extend far beyond that. He is the Founder and CEO of one of the biggest martial arts brands in the UK, with over 1,800 franchises worldwide. Meeting Matt was like a masterclass in discipline and focus. His relentless drive to grow his business and dedication to martial arts were truly inspiring. Talking to him, you could feel the intensity of his passion, and it was contagious. These weren't just people who had made it their way on their terms, which resonated deeply with me.

I could go on for ages about the incredible mentors I've had the privilege to learn from—if I were to include them all, this book would easily stretch to 1,000 pages! But let me highlight a few more names that have particularly resonated with me. For instance, there's Charlie Mullins, the founder of Pimlico Plumbers, whose entrepreneurial spirit and candid approach to business have truly inspired me. Then there's Simon Squibb, a serial entrepreneur and the founder of The Fortune Cookie Project; his insights on creativity and innovation in business are simply invaluable.

Rob Moore's perspectives on property investment and entrepreneurship have shifted my understanding of wealth-building. And how could I forget Nigel Farage? His boldness in political and business arenas has taught me the importance of standing firm in my beliefs and taking calculated risks.

Finally, Kevin Byrne, an expert in business growth strategies, has provided me with practical tools that have significantly impacted my approach to scaling my ventures.

These mentors, each with their unique backgrounds and expertise, have shaped my journey and expanded my horizons in ways I could never have anticipated.

The thing is, it was about more than just meeting successful people. It was also about all the other connections I made along the way and how they influenced my path. There was one time I remember when I planned to attend an event in London. I was excited about it, but fate had other plans. I made my way to London, but when I got to Croydon, there was a train strike that day, and no matter what I tried—bus, taxi, you name it—everything was full. Frustrated and out of options, I eventually decided to head back home.

On the way, I was chatting on a call with Darryl Lambert, a friend of mine from the millionaire mastermind group, and it turned out he had missed the event, too. We both felt a bit deflated, but we got to know that one of the expert speakers who was supposed to be at the London event was an international public speaker, and as luck would have it, he had offered us tickets to one of his upcoming events.

Without hesitation, we decided to make a weekend of it and attend his three-day event together.

That event turned out to be exactly what I needed. The speaker, Jessen James, hosted an event called "Unstoppable You," which was nothing short of transformative. For three days, the focus was entirely on personal growth, on discovering and understanding the past, accepting it, and then using that understanding to project and shape the future. The name of the event said it all, "Unstoppable You." Like Jessen James said at the event,

> “Step into your greatness.”

I walked out of that event feeling like a new person, with a clear vision of who I wanted to become and how I was going to get there.

Jessen James isn't just a speaker to me; he's like a brother. His mission is to change one billion lives, and after experiencing his event, I have no doubt he will achieve that goal. The knowledge he shares and the way he teaches are nothing short of life-changing. I owe so much to him for helping me get back on track and showing me what's possible when you focus on becoming the best version of yourself. That's the power of networking, my friends.

And here's the thing about networking that I've come to learn: It's not just about who you know; it's also about who knows you too. Building relationships is a two-way street, and it's crucial that others recognise your value as much as you realise theirs.

That's why, I've made it a priority to stay in touch with everyone I cross paths with. Whether it's a quick message, a phone call, or attending their events, I make sure that I maintain those connections. You never know where the next opportunity might come from or how someone you met years ago might be crucial to your journey.

A few months later, I found myself in Birmingham, attending one of the most transformative events of my life, Tony Robbins' Unleash the Power Within. It wasn't just a step up; it was a jump up, a leap into a whole new way of thinking and being. I was among 30,000 people gathered at the ECC, brimming with energy, passion, and a hunger for change. The event was nothing short of extraordinary.

For three days straight, from 8 am to 11 pm, I danced, I jumped, I pushed myself beyond what I thought were my limits, and I even did the fire walk. It was an experience out of this world. But what made it even more powerful were the connections I made. I met people who have since become friends, mentors, and collaborators. And the best part is that they're from all over the world: Germany, Iran, the USA, Brazil, Turkey, Singapore, and more.

Thanks to the power of networking, I now have a global community, people I can text or call, exchange ideas with, and support as they support me on our mutual paths to growth. As you can see, one more thing about networking isn't about advancing up the career ladder; it's about forming a community.

Networking involves surrounding yourself with individuals who motivate, challenge, and stand by you on your path to success. All achieving milestones feels more rewarding when cheered on by a tribe.

So, if there's one piece of advice I can give that has proven invaluable to me, it is that networking is a goldmine, but only if you nurture those relationships. Networking goes beyond being a tool you utilise when in need—it requires a shift in mindset. Imagine it as planting seeds. You can't just scatter seeds on the ground and expect a flourishing garden overnight. You need to water those seeds, nurture them and provide the environment for them to grow. Networking works in much the same way. It demands your time, effort and genuine interest to foster those connections.

So, it's not just about meeting people; it's about keeping in touch, staying engaged, and always being open to learning from them. Whether you're sending an email, reaching out on LinkedIn or meeting for lunch, staying in touch is crucial. I am glad I did. Aside from managing my business, I've always continued getting involved in networking activities. One critical thing to understand is that networking isn't just about what you can gain from others; it's also about what value you can add to them.

Occasionally, I lend a hand to others without any expectations, such as returning favours or simply nurturing friendships. It's not about gain; it's more about establishing relationships and standing by each other.

You see, every person you meet has a story, experiences, and lessons to share. By engaging in these conversations, you're not only expanding your network but also broadening your perspectives. You're gaining insights that can shape your decisions, challenge your thinking, and, ultimately, contribute to your growth. You never know, like me, when a missed train might lead you to the exact person or event that will change your life.

So, here's my challenge to you. Shift your perspective on networking. Instead of focusing on what you can get out of it, think about what you can give. Ask yourself, "How can I make an impact? How can I add value?"

When you approach networking with this mindset, the opportunities are limitless. The relationships you cultivate will not only enrich your life but will also create a ripple effect of positive impact far beyond what you might initially expect.

October 2023 had been a whirlwind. The Millionaire Mastermind event, which I'd been looking forward to for months, had ended. Without my network, the group of people I'd been bouncing ideas off of, sharing challenges with, and learning from, I needed a new adventure with like-minded people.

It was like finishing a puzzle only to discover there was one crucial piece missing. Networking. It was that missing piece, you know?

So, just before it finished, I did what any innovative entrepreneur would do. I searched online for a new community, a place where I could keep that momentum going. After hours of scrolling, browsing and reading reviews, it hit me. Why was I searching aimlessly when I had just spent an entire year with some of the most successful people in the industry?

I remembered to look back at the speakers from the Millionaire Mastermind event. That's when I discovered the MF.Club, led by none than Matt Fiddes himself. Yes, the same Matt Fiddes who once served as Michael Jackson's bodyguard and now excels in the martial arts industry. Intrigued, I decided to give it a shot. Right from my first group call, I sensed something special was in store.

Matt wasn't just sharing business advice in the way you might expect. He delivered hard-hitting truths, shared real-life experiences, and offered pure gold strategies. But what truly struck me was the atmosphere in the group. It felt like a family. Everyone was so supportive and open; we connected over our shared passion for business and personal development. It was a space where you could speak openly without fear of judgment. You know that feeling when you're with like-minded people? It's liberating!

Nobody felt lonely in their journey because we were all in it together, cheering each other on and sharing our challenges and victories. It made all the difference.

Being part of that community was a game-changer for me. Suddenly, I had access to a wealth of knowledge and experience, just a Zoom call away. It was like having my mentorship program on steroids. Every time I faced a challenge, I knew I had a group of people who would not only understand but offer actionable advice and encouragement. It wasn't just about the information; it was about the connection, the support, and the sense of belonging.

So, if you're feeling stuck in your business journey, do yourself a favour and find your community. Whether it's the MF.Club or another group that resonates with you, having that bond is truly invaluable. Trust me, when you find the right group, you'll know. It'll feel like you've found that missing piece of the puzzle, and suddenly, everything will start to click into place.

So, take that leap, reach out, and surround yourself with people who are as committed to their growth as you are to yours.

If the MF Club sounds like the right fit for you, You can use this link to sign up:
https://evaristo84--mfonline.thrivecart.com/mfpmn/.

Your future network and the success that comes with it are just one click away.

MASTER THE EQUATION OF SUCCESS

In Jack Canfield's The Success Principles, he introduces a simple yet profound formula: E + R = O.

This equation stands for Event + Response = Outcome.

This formula helps us understand how to handle life's situations. While we can't always control what happens to us (the events), we can control how we respond to those events. Our responses influence the results we get.

Let's look at a practical example. Imagine you need £100 to buy a train ticket. The event is that you need this money. The outcome is whether or not you get the ticket. Here's where your response comes in.

If you say, "I can't afford it," you're likely to end up without the ticket. But if you change your thinking to, "How can I afford it?" you start to see new options. Maybe you could sell five items for £20 each or one item for £100.

By taking this positive approach, you increase your chances of getting that train ticket.

This formula applies to every area of life, from finances to relationships, health, and even personal growth.

SO, LET'S SEE HOW YOU CAN SHIFT TO A MORE DYNAMIC MINDSET:

1. Shifting to a solution-driven mindset

Our minds are incredibly powerful problem-solving tools, but we often limit them with our language and thought patterns. We've all been there—facing a task, a goal, or a challenge that seems too big, too complicated, or too far out of reach. In those moments, the most common mindset people tend to have when faced with challenges is a limiting one: "I can't do this." It's like hitting a mental wall, closing off any possibility of a solution.

But here's the thing—what if, instead of accepting that you can't, you simply asked yourself, "How can I do this?" By changing that one word, you engage your subconscious mind, encouraging it to search for answers, dig deep into its resources, explore possibilities and develop creative solutions. It's like flipping a switch that allows creativity and problem-solving to flow. This shift in thinking is the foundation of a dynamic mindset.

Think of it as a muscle—the more you practice asking "how," the stronger your problem-solving ability becomes. This doesn't just happen overnight; it's a skill that grows with use. The more problems you approach with this mentality, the better you get at solving them, and as the problems you solve become more complex, so do the rewards.

2. Use the Power of your Subconscious Mind

One of the most fascinating aspects of our brains is the subconscious mind. Often, I'll meditate before bed on a specific issue or challenge, then allow myself to forget about it as I drift off to sleep. When I wake up, more often than not, the answer is there.

This isn't magic—it's the power of the subconscious mind. While sleeping, our brains continue to process information and look for solutions, often finding connections we might have missed while consciously thinking.

This technique is particularly useful when you feel stuck or unsure of how to respond to an event. By planting the seed of inquiry—asking yourself, "How can I solve this?"—you give your mind permission to work behind the scenes. When you wake up with a fresh perspective or a new idea, you've set yourself up for a different outcome.

3. Consider problems are opportunities in disguise

At the heart of the E + R = O equation I mentioned earlier is the idea that problems aren't to be feared—they're opportunities. The most successful people in life are those who excel at solving problems. They don't avoid challenges and don't sit around waiting for someone else to fix things.

Instead, they see problems as puzzles waiting to be solved.

It is never impossible to solve a problem. If you do not know how to solve them, seek help from others who can. Take something as simple as hanging a TV on the wall. You might not know how to do it yourself, so call a handyman to solve the problem for you. Or, say your boiler stops working, and you're left without hot water.

In that case, you'd probably call a gas engineer, who comes and fixes the issue. In both cases, the handyman and the gas engineer are problem solvers—professionals trained to respond to specific events with the right solutions. Without their help, you'd still be sitting there with a TV on the floor or no hot water. But because they've mastered their respective skills, they can fix the problem, and, in return, they charge for their expertise.

It's important to note that not all problems carry the same weight. Whether you're figuring out how to finance your dreams, navigate relationships, or improve your health or wealth, your ability to respond effectively to the events around you will determine your outcomes.

The bigger the problem, the bigger the reward for solving it. and the more skilled you become, the stronger your ability to tackle challenges, and the best part is the greater the benefits, too.

4. Having Broader Knowledge Matters

Our brains are like muscles the more you train, the stronger they become. Just like physical training builds strength, mental training improves problem-solving skills by creating more neural connections (the more neurocognitive). Of course, how you approach a problem can depend on your field of expertise, but I'd like to share some insights from my experience.

As I shared in Chapter 3, I'm a qualified gas engineer specialising in fixing boilers. But before entering this field, I spent over eight years as a qualified electrician and took courses in electronics and robotics. The reason I mention this is because my background in electrical work has been invaluable in helping me fully understand how boilers function. It's a perfect example of how knowing more than one subject can make problem-solving easier and more effective.

Let's take a completely different example—running a coffee shop. If you own a coffee shop, you'll need to learn how to make great coffee because the quality of your coffee will directly impact how many customers you attract. However, simply knowing how to brew coffee won't ensure the success of your business. There are many other aspects to consider: managing inventory, providing excellent customer service, keeping the place clean, handling paperwork (including taxes), and more.

I've seen many people open coffee shops, thinking their barista skills alone would carry them to success, only to close down within months after losing money. They may have mastered one element (making coffee) but lacked the broader understanding of running a business. The same principle applies to any field—whether you're running a business or solving complex problems, a well-rounded knowledge base gives you an edge.

5. Gaining Experience Before Taking the Leap

I worked as an employee for many years before starting my ventures, and I strongly advise anyone who is just starting out to do the same. Find a job in a field you're passionate about and learn everything you can while you're there.

If your long-term goal is to open a business in that field, the experience and knowledge you gain will be invaluable. Don't make the mistake of diving into business ownership without truly understanding how it works—you could end up losing both time and money.

In the UK, for instance, 20% of businesses close within the first year, and a staggering 60% shut down within three years. I believe that over 80% of these closures are due to business owners' lack of knowledge. Business isn't easy, but it becomes much more manageable when you understand how things work.

6. Delegate

You don't need to be an expert in every single aspect of your business. What's important is that you have a general understanding, which will allow you to delegate tasks effectively and oversee operations. When problems arise, this knowledge enables you to identify them early and either solve them yourself or guide your team toward a solution.

Another critical point: problem-solving doesn't have to be a solo activity. Leveraging your network can make things significantly easier. The phrase "your network is your net worth" holds true—having people to turn to for advice, support, or specialised expertise can be a game-changer when facing challenges.

Solving a problem doesn't have to involve going down alone; you will be better off using your network to help you solve problems, too.

7. Keep Progressing

Now, let's talk about progress. So often, we expect instant results. We want things to happen quickly; when they don't, it's easy to get discouraged and give up. But it is crucial to understand that progress is about taking those baby steps, and real, lasting growth often happens slowly, behind the scenes. Our impatience for results can lead us to give up just before reaching the finish line. I like to think about it in terms of the story of the bamboo tree.

When you plant a bamboo seed, nothing seems to happen for an entire year. In fact, it can take up to five years before you even see a tiny shoot emerge from the ground. But here's the amazing part—once that shoot breaks the surface, the bamboo can grow up to 90 feet tall in just six weeks. That's right—it can shoot up 39 inches in just 24 hours!

So, what's been going on during those five long, quiet years? The plant has been laying down deep, strong roots, preparing for its rapid growth. In many ways, our personal development is like that of a bamboo tree. We may be working hard, learning, growing, and making progress, but the results aren't always visible right away.

It can feel frustrating, especially when you're putting in the effort day after day without seeing immediate rewards. But just like the bamboo, real progress often happens beneath the surface in ways you might not notice at first. The key is patience. Trust that every small step, every tiny effort, is helping to lay the foundation for future success.

Remember that the journey isn't just about the result, it's about the transformation that happens along the way. And that transformation starts with a single shift in mindset.

As you can see now, personal and professional growth is a continuous journey that involves cultivating self-awareness, developing new skills, and evolving in response to the challenges we face.

Whether in our personal lives or in our careers, this growth is a fundamental part of who we become.

As we approach the end of this chapter, I want to share with you three important lessons that completely changed my life. These lessons reshaped how I approach my business, life, relationships, and even mindset. They are simple yet profoundly impactful ideas that can lead to significant growth. Let's explore them one by one.

1. SHIFT FROM SELLING TO SERVING

One of the most transformative lessons I've learned in the business world is the shift from a "selling" mindset to a "serving" mindset. At first glance, it may seem similar, but this powerful concept is vastly different in approach and impact. I first heard this concept from my friend and mentor, Jessen James, who often says,

> Don't sell to people; help them to buy.

That single phrase completely reframed how I approach business. When your primary goal is to sell, it's easy to push your product or service onto others, even if they don't truly need it. You may even see your customers as numbers or transactions rather than real people with real needs. This approach can create friction and a lack of trust and may even damage relationships in the long run.

However, everything changes when you shift your focus from simply making sales to genuinely helping people. You become less of a salesperson and more of a trusted advisor. Your goal is no longer just to close the deal but to provide real value by solving problems and offering solutions that improve the lives of the people you serve.

The reality is that people are constantly searching for answers. Whether selecting the right product, overcoming obstacles or reaching personal or professional goals, there's always a demand for assistance and direction. And guess what? If you have the solution they're looking for, it creates a win-win situation for everyone involved. They get the help they need, and you get to make a sale.

And here's the best part – when you create a win-win situation, you become the go-to person or business they trust—someone they return to and recommend to others.

That's why, even when you feel pressured to focus on making sales, it's important to pause and ask yourself, "How can I genuinely help this person? What challenges are they facing, and how can I contribute positively to their situation?"

By serving first, you'll naturally build more profound, authentic relationships and sales will follow.

2. SHIFT FROM BEING A CONSUMER TO CREATOR

There was a moment when Matt Fiddes said something that completely shifted how I saw myself and approached life. He told me, "Be a creator, not a consumer." It was like a light bulb moment for me. Instead of absorbing content made by others, why not shape our own stories and design our destinies by creating and posting our content, whether it's sharing knowledge, creating art, building a business, or simply putting our thoughts out there?

Think about it—how often do we consume without really contributing? We spend hours absorbing other people's work, their ideas, and their accomplishments, but what if we flipped that script?

Most of the time, people don't know who you are or what you do, and then you find yourself complaining that you can't help people with what you do! Does that ring a bell? I know I've been there, feeling like I had so much to offer, but no one seemed to notice. The reality is that people won't see what you're capable of until you show them. That's the magic of shifting from passive consumers to active creators. It's an impactful change in mindset that will transform your life and inspire those around you.

When you prioritise creation over consumption, you set standards and demonstrate your true capabilities to the world. You become someone who takes in information and gives back, contributing value in your own unique way.

People start to notice. You begin to build a presence, a brand, and an identity that reflects what you stand for and what you're passionate about.

And here's the thing—most people are too wrapped up in their own lives to realise what you're doing unless, so how do you make people know what you're all about? It is simple, take action. Each day, in small or big ways, you can share your talents, skills, and interests with the world. You don't have to wait for the perfect moment or until you feel 100% ready. Start now with what you have, as Jack Canfield once told me,

> "Start now and get perfect later."

The more you create and share, the more you become a beacon of hope, positivity, and inspiration in a world that can often feel gloomy or uncertain.

Now, I am not going to lie. I've found that when I'm deep in consuming content—whether it's mindlessly scrolling through Instagram or watching another YouTube video—there's a nagging feeling that I'm not living up to my potential. It's like I'm just sitting on the sidelines, watching others live their lives instead of actively shaping my own.

Have you ever felt that way?

Next time you catch yourself deep in consumption mode, ask yourself, "Am I living up to my true potential right now? Am I sharing my talents with the world in a meaningful way?"

And if the answer is no, don't get down on yourself—instead, think about what small steps you can take today to start creating. It doesn't have to be something big. It could be as simple as sharing your thoughts in a blog post, recording a short video, designing something new, or brainstorming ideas for a project you've been putting off.

Trust me, when you shift from consumer to creator, you manifest the life you've always dreamed of. You stop being a spectator and start being the architect of your own story.

3. THERE IS MATH BEHIND THE MAGIC.

Now, take a moment to think about the last time you faced something daunting—maybe it was a big project at work, a personal goal like learning a new skill, or even something as simple as organising a cluttered space. At first glance, these tasks can feel overwhelming, but the reality is they're never truly insurmountable. They just need to be broken down into manageable steps. And sometimes, the first step is as simple as asking for help, seeking advice, or delegating tasks.

The important thing is not giving up when things feel too hard. Instead, focus on finding ways to tackle the challenge in front of you, piece by piece.

An old saying sums this up perfectly:

> "If you think you can or cannot do it, guess what!
> You are right."

This wisdom reminds us that our beliefs shape our outcomes. As I mentioned, if you truly believe you're capable of something, your brain will work on figuring out how to make it happen. But if you believe you can't, you've already decided the outcome before you've even started.

Achieving ambitious goals requires more than wishful thinking; it demands a strategic mindset and a deep alignment with your goals. Let's say your aim is to earn £1 million in a year. That sounds difficult to achieve, right? At first glance, this might seem like a massive, impossible, daunting and unrealistic target. However, think for a moment about what would happen if you broke it down into smaller, more digestible steps. Suddenly, you'll discover this seemingly unrealistic goal becoming far more manageable and achievable.

First and foremost, before diving into the breakdown, there's one fundamental thing you need to do is 'believe'. Without genuinely believing that your goal is attainable, no amount of planning or effort will propel you forward. Think of it like this: if you don't believe the goal is within your grasp, your brain will subtly sabotage your efforts.

Once you shift your mindset to truly see this goal as achievable, you've already taken a crucial first step toward success.

Then, the next most important step is to start breaking down the goal. Now, let's deconstruct the £1 million target to understand how it can be achieved. Instead of letting yourself get overwhelmed by the big number, you can break it down into smaller, more manageable pieces that give you a clearer view of the path ahead.

Okay, it is time to start breaking it down and see the math behind the magic.

Let's begin with the £1 million yearly target and work our way backwards:

- Yearly Goal: £1,000,000
- Monthly Goal: Divide £1,000,000 by 12 months, which gives you approximately £83,333 per month.
- Daily Goal: Next, divide the monthly goal by the average number of working days in a month, let's say 20. This results in about £4,166 per day.
- Hourly Goal: Assuming you work 8 hours a day, divide the daily goal by 8. This means you'll need to make around £520 per hour.

Now, I know what you're thinking. These numbers may still seem high, but by breaking them down further, you can start to see how to make them more approachable.

Let's say you're selling a product or service. If your product is priced at £20 per unit, you'd need to sell 26 units per hour to hit that £520 hourly goal. If your product is higher-priced, let's say £260 per unit, you'd only need to sell 2 units per hour. Suddenly, the task starts to look a lot more realistic.

This approach works with more than just sales. Whether your goal involves financial targets, completing a big project, or achieving personal milestones, breaking it down into smaller steps helps to demystify the process. You begin to see the path, and instead of one huge mountain to climb, you're tackling it step by step, foothold by foothold.

Of course, as you may have realised from my experiences, life rarely goes according to plan. Not every hour or day will be the same. Some hours will be more productive than others, and sales will fluctuate. And that's perfectly normal. The key is to maintain an average that keeps you on track toward your overall goal.

Flexibility is crucial here—be open to adjusting your approach as you learn more about what works best. If sales are slower in the morning but pick up in the afternoon, adjust your focus to capitalise on those peak hours.

Now that you can see the benefit of breaking down your goals in terms of numbers let's see what's really happening when you break down big goals like this.

You see, this exercise is more than just a mathematical breakdown—it's a shift in perspective. By rethinking how you approach significant goals, you start to see the world differently, making the impossible seem possible. It's a mindset shift that transforms intimidation into empowerment. This approach can be applied to any goal, whether it's financial, personal, or professional.

The key takeaway is that big dreams aren't out of reach—they're just a series of smaller tasks waiting to be tackled.

So, by aligning your mindset with your goals and breaking them down into smaller, manageable tasks, you create a powerful system for success. Ask any successful person, and they will tell you the same thing: It transforms seemingly impossible targets into achievable milestones. They understand that reaching big targets is built on daily progress, small wins, and consistent effort.

You can turn your ambitions into reality by understanding and believing in the possibility of success and systematically working towards it. This way of thinking not only boosts your confidence but also provides a clear roadmap to achieving your dreams.

I call it a Dynamic Mindset!

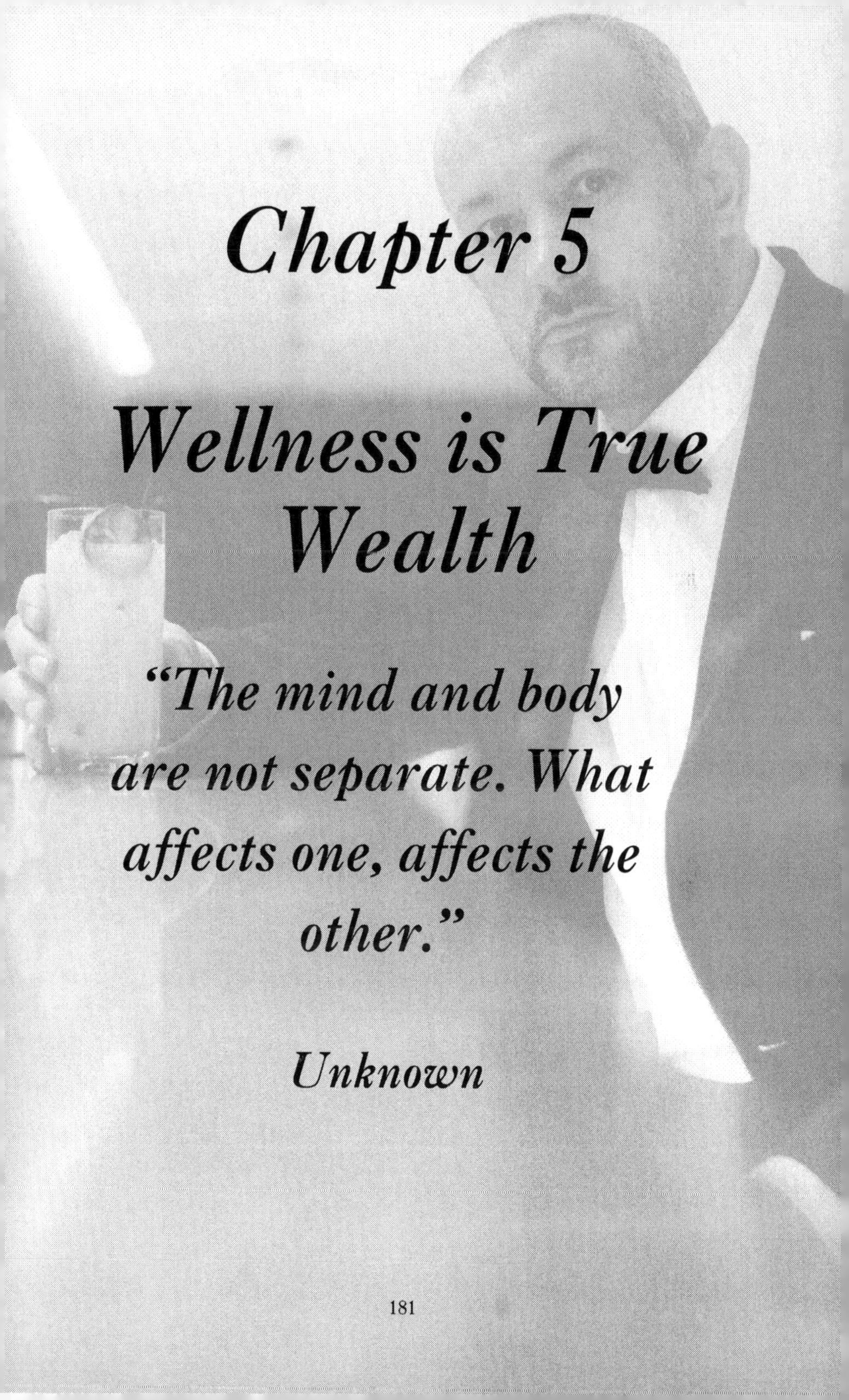

Chapter 5

Wellness is True Wealth

"The mind and body are not separate. What affects one, affects the other."

Unknown

WELLNESS IS TRUE WEALTH

In the previous chapters, we delved into the inner strength that helps us weather life's storms, the pressures and obligations that often feel overwhelming, and the courage to embrace uncertainty. We also examined how growth, both personal and professional, is intertwined with challenges and transformation. Now, we turn our focus inward; toward the foundation that sustains it all: our well-being.

When I started taking ownership, I soon realised that I had fallen into the trap that so many of us do, associating success with money and happiness with possessions. I believed that if I could earn, buy, and achieve more, I would finally feel fulfilled. But as I navigated through life, drowning my sorrows in alcohol and chasing after every shiny object that came my way, I was confronted with a harsh reality: no amount of riches could fill the emptiness inside me.

No achievements or recognition could compensate for my lack of purpose and contentment. It served as a wake-up call, reminding me that true wealth is not measured by bank balances but by the depth of our experiences and connections.

I had been so focused on external success, building my career, accumulating possessions, and climbing the ladder that I had completely neglected the inner work that needed to be done.

My mindset, values, and sense of self were all out of alignment. I was striving for something that was always out of reach, never realising that what I was searching for couldn't be found in the material world. I started to understand that I needed to make changes not in my business endeavours but in my mindset; despite my efforts, the void persisted. I was trapped in a cycle of striving and seeking something beyond my grasp.

This realisation sparked a deeper exploration into what true fulfilment really looks like. I began to understand that success isn't just about what we achieve externally; it's also about how we feel internally. We often overlook the importance of nurturing our mental, emotional, and physical health in pursuit of our goals.

In this chapter, we'll dive into how wellness and success are connected and show how taking care of ourselves in a holistic way can lead to more resilience, clarity, and joy. Whether it's finding mental peace, focusing on physical health, or seeing self-care as a form of strength, wellness is the foundation of a meaningful life. When we prioritise our well-being, we truly thrive in every part of our journey. So, if you aim to create real wealth, it may mean making significant changes!

To help guide you, let's take a closer look at what "real wealth" really means.

THE REAL WEALTH

Most people misunderstand the meaning of wealth. When I ask others what wealth means, the typical responses revolve around "Having lots of money, assets, or passive income." If you search for the definition online, you'll find a similar answer: "An abundance of valuable possessions or money." This aligns with what most people think when they hear the word "wealth."

But let me ask you a quick question. Have you ever thought of what matters more in your life? For instance, what is the point of having all the success and money in the world if you don't have health, love, good emotions, family, good friendships and a fulfilling life?

You see, I, too, used to believe that being wealthy meant having lots of money and plenty of free time. But my understanding of wealth has evolved over the years—it's now so much more than just a big bank account. True wealth isn't just about material success or the things we achieve. It goes much deeper—it's found in the health of our mind, body, and spirit.

Wealth, to me, is about everything that surrounds you.

It's not only about having a large sum of money but also about creating a financial environment that's stable and sustainable, one that can withstand life's inevitable ups and downs. Most importantly, wealth is about focusing on what truly matters to you.

For some people, time might be more valuable than money. You may prefer to spend your time with loved ones, pursuing hobbies, or simply taking time to relax and recharge. That doesn't mean money isn't important—it definitely has its place. But it does highlight the need for a balance between different aspects of life to truly feel wealthy.

This balance is key, and a practical way to think about it is the 8+8+8 rule, which I discussed in Chapter 2. The idea is to divide your day into three equal parts: eight hours for work, eight hours for sleep, and eight hours for the 3F, 3H, and 3S. By structuring your day this way, you can create a more balanced and fulfilling life where you make time not only for your career but also for yourself and the people who matter to you.

This is true wealth!

FOCUS ON ONE MASTERPIECE AT A TIME

Life is what we create. It is like painting a massive mural—you're the artist, and your decisions are the brushstrokes. Now, imagine yourself as if you are the Michelangelo of your own life. You are constantly crafting your unique masterpiece. Sounds fancy, right? I mean, have you seen the Sistine Chapel? That took years, and that guy probably didn't have Twitter or Netflix constantly fighting for his attention!

The truth is, every thought, action, and decision you make is like a brushstroke on your canvas. The more deliberate and focused you are, the more your masterpiece becomes more detailed and meaningful. Similarly, what you think and focus on today shapes the reality you will live in tomorrow. This sounds pretty powerful, right? But guess what? The best part is that this power lies within your hands. Therefore, you cannot expect a masterpiece overnight because some paintings take more time to come to life, and it all depends on the effort and actions you put into creating your vision.

Now, to reinforce this, try imagining yourself starting a painting. When you begin, you might have a clear idea of what you want to create and even a grand vision. But as you work on it, a happy little accident happens, and sometimes the picture changes. And that's okay because the goal is to start painting and see it through to completion. Just as a painter works diligently on one piece before starting another, It's the same with life.

A painter doesn't jump from one half-finished canvas to the next, hoping to create a bunch of scattered masterpieces. No, they focus, brushstroke by brushstroke, until their vision is complete.

When it comes to business, it's often said that quality beats quantity. Think about it: isn't it better to have one truly successful business, something you can focus your energy on and grow, rather than juggling three or four that are just mediocre? Focusing on a single venture allows you to dedicate more time, energy, and resources to its success, leading to deeper expertise, better customer satisfaction, and, ultimately, greater long-term rewards. When you spread yourself too thin, it's hard to give any of them the attention they deserve, and in the end, none of them really flourish.

The same logic applies to personal life, too. For instance, wouldn't you agree that having a healthy body—feeling strong, energised, and at your best—is far more valuable than just being "okay" physically? It's about being able to live life fully rather than just getting by.

The point is that life requires that same kind of focus. If you're hopping between projects, trying to do it all at once, everything ends up looking like a giant, colourful mess. Concentrate on one thing at a time, and you'll find your work—whether it's a project, business or your life—turns out way more satisfying.

Sounds simple, right?

But let's be honest—how many of us are guilty of trying to juggle a hundred things at once? And the result?

Stress, chaos, and that wonderful feeling of spinning your wheels but not getting anywhere. Can you relate to this? Because I definitely can. I've experienced this firsthand.

For years, I was constantly busy, always 'doing,' but I wasn't making much real progress at the end of the day. I hit a glass ceiling, and it felt like no matter how fast I moved, I couldn't break through. It was like running on a treadmill with lots of movement but zero distance. I wasn't growing or evolving in my personal and professional life.

Then it hit me: I was so wrapped up in trying to do everything that I'd completely neglected the most crucial part of the equation—myself.

My mind was cluttered, my body was running on fumes, and I had completely ignored the fact that mental clarity and personal wellness are the foundation for growth. You can't build anything—be it a career, a relationship, or even a hobby—on a shaky foundation, right? And mine was practically quicksand. So, I had to take a step back, get off the hamster wheel, and think: 'What's the point of being busy if it's not actually moving me forward?'

That's when I realised the obvious but often overlooked truth: if I didn't invest in my own mental and physical wellness, I'd remain stuck. Like, permanently.

In fact, personal well-being acts as the fuel that drives all other aspects of life, including productivity and creativity. When your mind is cluttered, or your body is unwell, achieving goals, maintaining focus, or making sound decisions becomes difficult. Prioritising mental and physical health ensures that you're operating at your full potential, whether in your personal life or professional endeavours.

HEALTH BEFORE WEALTH

I've spoken with several multimillionaire friends who say they would give away all their money to have their parents back. While we know that's not possible, their sentiments reveal a more profound truth: there are things far more critical to a human being than money. You could spend your youth pushing your limits, sacrificing sleep, and abusing your health and peace of mind to get rich. You might think it's worth it, that the rewards will justify the toll it takes on your body and mind.

But what happens years down the line when you're spending all that hard-earned money trying to reclaim the health you lost along the way?

Or, you could spend all your time and energy on your career, obsessively pursuing financial success. You're so focused on the next promotion, the next big deal, that you don't notice you've neglected yourself, your family, and your friends. You don't see the moments you've missed, the birthdays, the quiet dinners, the simple joys of being present.

One day, you might find yourself surrounded by the symbols of success, a big house, a fancy car, and a hefty bank account, but this can often lead to loneliness and depression.

So, was it really worth it? That's a high price to pay for a fat bank account, don't you think?

These examples are just a few of the countless reasons why I believe that wealth is more than just money or possessions. Imagine living a life where you have the freedom to travel, immerse yourself in the world's beauty, experience different cultures, and share these moments with the people who matter most to you. That, to me, is the essence of wealth. It's not just about the financial security to afford these experiences but also having the health, energy, time, and meaningful relationships to fully enjoy them. It's the ability to balance your responsibilities and desires, pursue your passions, and live a rich life in every sense of the word.

One day, one of my mentors I mentioned in Chapter 4, Matt Fiddes, shared something that has stuck with me ever since:

> "Health before wealth."

At first, it seemed like a simple phrase, but the more I thought about it, the more it made sense. As I mentioned earlier, I started reflecting and asking myself, what's the point of accumulating wealth if you're not healthy enough to enjoy it?

Taking care of yourself is so important. That advice became a turning point in my life, and from that moment on, I made a commitment to prioritise my health. I've realised that prioritising my mental well-being has empowered me to achieve things I once thought were completely out of reach. Allow me to share my story to illustrate this point.

As a gas engineer, I used to install a few boilers every month. Now, you wouldn't think much of it at first, but these boilers, weighing an average of 30kg each, weren't exactly the easiest to handle, especially when it came to mounting them on walls. It was a physical challenge, and to be honest, it took a toll on my body. I'd often find myself dealing with aches and pains, which made an already demanding job even tougher.

Years ago, though, I made a decision that I'd been putting off for a while—I joined a gym. You see, hitting the gym throughout my life wasn't really my thing. It wasn't until 2019 that I finally decided to give it a try and signed up at a local gym. Initially, I saw some changes after going for about three months. However, when my friend lost interest and stopped joining, I also lost motivation. When I stopped going, I lost my momentum.

The thing is, it is the same in all areas of life; excuses are procrastination and often serve as a way to delay tasks, diverting our attention to the simple ones instead of those that truly make a difference.

It's typically the tasks you tend to avoid that drive you forward. Like Jessen James says,

> “Pain is temporary, quitting lasts forever.”

Last year, I gave it another shot, and this time around, it stuck with me. To be honest, I'd always had this idea that gyms were for people who wanted to get big, you know, those massive bodybuilder types. But I quickly realised that I had it all wrong. My goal wasn't to bulk up to that extent. I wasn't looking to become a bodybuilder or anything like that; my aim was to build some muscle, improve my strength, and, more importantly, take better care of my overall health and well-being, especially with the physical demands of my job.

I started eating healthier, exercising regularly, and taking better care of myself overall. The transformation I've experienced over the past year has been nothing short of remarkable. I'm not just talking about physical changes, although those are significant, but I had more energy, better focus, a body that feels stronger and more capable and how I feel throughout the day. Hoisting those hefty boilers became surprisingly more manageable.

My experience at the gym taught me that regular exercise extends beyond muscle development; it is integral to holistic wellness.

I felt more robust, invigorated and better equipped to tackle the demands of my profession. The mental and emotional benefits have been just as profound.

Procrastination, which used to plague me, has almost disappeared from my life, and so many things that used to feel like a struggle now seem easier and more manageable. I used to think going to the gym was a waste of time, something I had to force myself to do. Now, it's a non-negotiable part of my routine. The gym is more than just a place to work out; it's a sanctuary. Sure, I go there to stay fit, but it's also where I unwind, reflect on my day and plan for tomorrow. While lifting weights or jogging on the treadmill, I often work through problems or develop new ideas.

For me, it's a moment of freedom where I can think and process thoughts without distractions. What I've noticed, though, is that a lot of people at the gym are glued to their phones between sets, texting or scrolling through apps. Even though they're physically there, their minds seem preoccupied with the chaos of life. By not giving themselves that mental break from constant information and tasks, it's no surprise they feel stuck or struggle to move forward. I think the gym can be so much more than a fitness space—it can be a mental escape, too, if you let it.

Our brain is like a machine; optimum performance occurs when it operates smoothly with rest intervals.

Like a machine that overheats if it runs continuously without breaks, our brains suffer when deprived of rest, be it sufficient sleep or downtime. Therefore, incorporating mental breaks is essential. When we sleep, our brains have the opportunity to process information, form neural connections, and store memories. This processing aids in our learning and problem-solving capabilities.

When I am working on important tasks at home or at my office, or when I am at the gym, I leave my phone in the locker or set it on silent mode. This way, I can concentrate on my workout. This provides my mind with the space to relax and think creatively. This habit has impacted how I solve problems and maintain mental clarity.

You see, now, my drive comes from within me. I've come to value the mental advantages of a workout routine, turning it into a personal commitment, and now going to the gym has become a part of my routine. Typically, I would head to the gym five days a week in the evenings, engaging in a 45-minute workout session followed by an hour of swimming and relaxing in the sauna or steam room. This routine not only keeps me in shape but also helps me unwind after a long day.

I've realised that on days when I skip my gym, I tend to feel more tired and struggle with falling asleep at night. It's like my body craves that physical activity. I have to admit, though, that it is tough sometimes; there are times when I lack motivation to go; however, setting goals requires pushing through excuses. Those are precisely the moments when pushing myself is most crucial. Interestingly enough, pushing through those moments often leads to a productive workout session once I'm there, andif something comes up and I miss a session, I make it up on my next day off. It’s become part of who I am, a habit that reinforces my commitment to myself every day.

This shift in mindset isn't just about hitting the gym or eating better. It's about understanding that life is meant to be lived, not just survived. We all have responsibilities—family, work, and community—but within those, we have to carve out time for ourselves to do what truly makes us happy.

> “ Life is short, and we are responsible for making the most of it! ”

Think about what you really want out of life, not just what you think you should want. What are the things that light you up inside? Who are the people you want to spend your time with?

Once you have those answers, go after them with everything you've got.

MASTERING YOUR SCHEDULE

Now, our world is getting so fast-paced that the one thing we all have in common is the constant feeling that there's never enough time. Between work, family, social obligations, self-care, and personal goals, it can feel like you're always racing the clock. Sound familiar? Trust me, I get it. Life pulls you in a thousand directions, and finding balance can seem like a myth. So, let's start by shifting how we think about time.

Most people treat time like it's something that's constantly slipping away. You've probably heard the saying, "You have the same 24 hours in a day as Beyoncé." Well, that's true, but let's be honest—Beyoncé also has a team of people helping her manage those 24 hours. We may not all have assistants (or the bank account to hire them), but we can take control of how we spend our days. And once you master that, your life can truly change.

Do it not just for yourself but for your family, your friends, and your community. Because when you're living a life that fulfils you, that joy radiates out and touches everyone around you.

You see, I've lived in the UK for the past 16 years, and during that time, we've tried to bring my parents here to live with us. They visited us on holiday, but they've made it clear they prefer staying in Madeira.

At first, I struggled with their decision because I wanted them close to me and to be a more significant part of their daily lives. But then I realised that this was their choice, their happiness, and I needed to respect that. So, I've visited them twice a year for the past five years. I also make sure to call them two or three times a week. Staying connected to them is a priority for me because I know how precious time is.

My siblings often joke that I'm the favourite child, and while I laugh it off, it is actually true. It's not because I'm better than them or because I've made an effort to be present in my parents' lives. I know their joys and struggles; I'm just a phone call away whenever they need me. It's a role I've taken on willingly, and I'll do whatever it takes to make their lives easier. There's something profoundly fulfilling about being there for the people who have always been there for you. My parents are healthy now, and I'm grateful for that, but I'm also acutely aware that time marches on, and there will come a day when they're no longer here. I don't want to look back with regrets, wishing I had spent more time with them.

Love you, Mum and Dad.

Thank you for being the reason I strive to be my best every day.

Okay, let's get back to mastering your schedule. You see it is less about having more time and more about making the most of the time you already have. And believe me, when you get this down, it's like unlocking a superpower. However, it's not just about productivity but your overall well-being. While we often focus on getting things done, it's just as crucial to ensure we're taking care of ourselves. Without prioritising well-being, no amount of time management will truly feel satisfying. Finding a balance between hustle and self-care is essential. This means scheduling your tasks and creating space for rest, reflection, and renewal.

Think of it this way: managing your time effectively is one of the most powerful tools for protecting your mental and emotional health. It gives you control over your day instead of letting the day control you. This can reduce stress, anxiety, and that overwhelming feeling that you're perpetually behind. When you carve out time for things that nourish your body and soul—like exercise, mindfulness, hobbies, or simply breathing—you feel better and become more resilient and focused.

Well-being isn't just something to squeeze in when everything else is done; it should be integrated into how we approach life. The more intentional you are with your time, the more energy you have to bring your best self to every area of life, whether it's your work, relationships, or personal growth.

So, instead of chasing after more hours in the day, aim to use the ones you have to support your goals and well-being. Because at the end of the day, thriving in life is about more than just checking off boxes—it's about feeling fulfilled, energised, and at peace with how you spend your time.

Have you ever heard the saying, "What gets scheduled gets done "? It's a mantra that highlights the importance of having a schedule. However, there's a catch: making a schedule is one thing, but sticking to it is another challenge.

Imagine you have your day meticulously planned out, every hour accounted for. Then unexpectedly, a significant situation arises—something that deeply resonates with you, elicits high emotion, or sparks passion within you. Suddenly, your motives and that crafted schedule go out the window—your action changes, impacting the outcome you expected.

So, what's the solution? It's all about striking a balance between structure and flexibility. This is where colour-coded schedules become useful.

Visualise your schedule enhanced with colours. Red is for tasks that need urgent attention, Amber is for tasks that require completion today, Blue is for tasks to wrap up by week's end, and Green is for monthly projects. With this system of organisation, you can easily spot what requires attention and what can be put off for later. It's like having a traffic signal for your list of tasks, guiding you through the chaos of life. Alright, let's break it down in more detail.

RED

When a task is marked in red on your schedule, that's your cue to stop everything and take action; you need to address it urgently. Whether the task is simple or a more significant challenge you've been dreading, it must be handled ASAP. And here's the thing: occasionally, a relaxed task labelled in blue or another colour suddenly becomes red due to time constraints or altered circumstances.

What's interesting, though, is that a red task on our schedule never changes to blue or another colour. The moment it turns red, that's it; you've got to make it your top priority. Think of it as a stop sign: whatever else you were working on can wait because this task just jumped to the front of the line.

Once it hits red, there's no going back to blue or green. Often, those red tasks are the ones you've probably been avoiding because they are complex or you don't feel like doing them, right? Maybe it's something you don't want to deal with because it feels overwhelming, or you don't feel like doing it. That's why it turns red. When it was any other colour, we probably pushed it off, thinking, "Oh, I've got time," or "I'll get to that later." But guess what? Later has arrived, and now there's no escaping it.

So, when a task turns red, it's go-time. No more excuses and no more procrastination. It's time to buckle down and just get it done.

You might not like it, but trust me, the relief and satisfaction you'll feel once you tackle it are so worth it. Red tasks force you to take control, and by addressing them head-on, you're not just managing your schedule—you're managing your life.

AMBER

When we have an Amber task on the schedule, it's like a big warning signal flashing at us, saying, "You better deal with this soon!" It's less urgent than a red task, but it's definitely creeping up on you. An Amber task is usually something we've been putting off for days, maybe even longer. You know the type—those things we keep pushing to the next day because we think, "I'll get to it tomorrow." Well, now time's running out.

The trick with Amber's tasks is that they can't be ignored for too long. They got to be completed on the same day, without any excuses or delays. No "ifs," "ands," or "buts." Amber tasks are like the last warning before things get serious, so when you see one, that's your sign to take action. You've got a window—until 3 p.m., for example—but once that time passes, the task escalates into a red one. And as we've discussed earlier, once a task turns red, there's no going back. You can't demote it to blue or green.

It's in the red zone, and at that point, it becomes an urgent, must-do-now kind of task. That's why Amber tasks are so important to tackle before they spiral out of control.

BLUE

When we see a blue colour-coded task on our, it's like a gentle nudge saying, "Hey, make sure you complete me sometime this week." These tasks are the ones we've designated for the week's checklist. Nothing too urgent, but they still need to be completed before the week's over. They serve as helpful reminders, keeping us on track without stressing us out.

The beauty of blue tasks is that they're not pressing, so if there are any Red or Amber tasks demanding our attention, those take priority. But here's where it gets interesting: by the time Thursday rolls around, that relaxed blue task starts to shift—it gets bumped up to Amber status. Suddenly, there's a sense of urgency.

But don't worry! Most of the time, we're ahead of schedule and finish those tasks well before Thursday arrives. With an entire week to tackle them, blue tasks usually feel pretty manageable. We can break them into smaller parts, working on them bit by bit at our own pace. That's the advantage of blue tasks—they give us the flexibility to handle our workload without feeling overwhelmed.

They act as gentle prompts to keep us on course, making sure we're moving forward without the pressure that comes with Amber or Red tasks. The trick is to not let them sit there for too long, though.

It's easy to look at a blue task and think, "I've got all week," but that's where people can slip up. So, consider blue tasks your opportunity to stay ahead of the game. They're like little checkpoints that keep you moving in the right direction, offering just enough structure to keep things flowing smoothly without adding extra pressure.

The key is using that flexibility wisely to manage your time efficiently.

GREEN

When we glance at a green task on our calendar, it serves as a guiding light that leads us towards our monthly objectives. Green tasks aren't as urgent as the others—they give us more breathing room—but they still represent important milestones we need to hit before the month's over. Ideally, we strive to complete these green tasks within the first three weeks of the month.

However, if three weeks pass without any progress, that green task is changed to the status of a blue task on our schedule. It acts as a nudge, reminding us not to overlook it! So, while green tasks offer flexibility, they require monitoring to ensure they don't slip through the cracks and become last-minute rush jobs.

The key is to stay aware of them, even if they're not immediately demanding your attention.

Now, when it comes to keeping this system running smoothly, I've found that reviewing my schedule every morning makes a huge difference. Before diving into the day's activities, I like to glance over what's on my plate. It helps me mentally prepare and prioritise, especially if there are any red tasks that need immediate focus. Additionally, I can rearrange things as necessary and adjust priorities on the go. It's like having a roadmap for the day, ensuring I'm focused on what truly matters.

In the evenings, I do a quick review as well. I like to go over what I've accomplished, check off what's been completed, and move those finished tasks into the "done" section. It's a bit like tidying up loose ends, making sure nothing gets overlooked before the day is officially done. It's also really satisfying to see your progress laid out in front of you—it motivates you to keep going.

Here's the thing, though: no system is perfect. We're all human, and sometimes life gets in the way. Maybe you're feeling lazy, or you've had a long day, and sticking to the system feels like too much. It happens! The real question is, what is the solution when the system breaks down?

The solution isn't to beat yourself up over a missed task or an off day. Instead, it's about having a plan for those moments. The best way to recover is to be flexible and forgiving with yourself. Remember, mastering your schedule isn't about squeezing every minute out of the day.

It's about creating a life where your time aligns with your values and priorities. It's about finding balance, setting boundaries, and making space for what really matters. Therefore, if you fall off track, the key is to reset—take a few minutes the following day or evening to review where you stand, identify what needs immediate attention, and get back into the rhythm.

So, take a deep breath. You've got this!

Start small, make it personal, and remember: the goal is progress, not perfection. Once you learn to master your schedule, you'll find yourself with more energy, more focus, and more time for the things that make your life truly rich. Because at the end of the day, wellness is wealth—and time, when managed wisely, is one of your most significant investments.

REWARD YOURSELF

By now, you've embraced the Red, Amber, Blue and Green schedule strategy as a tool to manage your time and increase productivity. But there's one crucial aspect we still need to cover: the importance of celebrating your success. Before we dive into that, let me share where I used to mess up. I was constantly rewarding myself for the small, inconsequential tasks that didn't push me toward my bigger goals. Whether it was checking off an item on my to-do list or completing a minor errand, I always found an excuse to treat myself. And do you know what happened?

Most of the time, the important tasks—the ones that really mattered—were left unfinished. This cycle of prematurely rewarding myself left me feeling unsatisfied, frustrated, and stagnant. Despite doing "something" every day, I wasn't actually moving forward in the ways I wanted to. That's when I knew something had to change.

I set a new rule for myself: No rewards until the important tasks, my "Red" tasks, were completed. If I had three crucial things to do that day, I could not celebrate, relax, or enjoy any form of reward until they were done. It was tough at first—breaking the habit of instant gratification is never easy—but slowly, it started to make a difference.

Suddenly, the rewards felt earned.

They became a reminder of how much progress I had made and how far I had come. That well-deserved reward, whether it was relaxing with a movie or enjoying my favourite meal, became a symbol of real achievement. It was no longer a moment of fleeting satisfaction but a meaningful celebration of hard work. So, before we move on to the next section, I want to leave you with two simple but powerful tips.

First, celebrate your successes, but only when they're truly earned. Save your rewards for when you've completed the important work and when you've moved the needle on your goals. Let those celebrations be meaningful, a symbol of persistence and progress.

Second, keep your perspective in check. Don't get so caught up in the small tasks that you lose sight of the bigger picture. Use the Red, Amber, Blue and Green strategy to manage your time, but remember—life isn't just about checking off tasks. It's about moving toward something greater, something more meaningful.

Take a step back when you need to. Look at the entire puzzle, not just the individual pieces. Ask yourself whether the activities you're engaging in are helping you build the life you truly want or are just filling time. When you embrace these ideas, not only will you become more productive, but you'll also find deeper satisfaction in the journey. You'll have a clearer sense of purpose, and your rewards will feel all the sweeter for it.

Now, go out there and make things happen. You've got the tools, mindset, and strategy—use them well. Celebrate when the time is right, and keep your eyes on the bigger picture. The outcomes will show for themselves.

SUCCESS SIMPLIFIED

Now, let me tell you a few little secrets about success—it's not just about talent or luck. In fact, while those things can give you a head start, they're not what truly defines success. The real key to turning your dreams into reality lies in something much simpler yet incredibly powerful: discipline, practice, always do your best and persistence.

These four pillars are the foundation of any meaningful achievement, no matter what you're aiming for. Let's explore how you can master these principles to unlock your true potential, whether it's your career, health, or personal goals.

Discipline:

Having a plan is one thing, but sticking to it? That's a whole other challenge. But turning your dreams into reality is totally doable, with a thing called discipline. It's one of those life rules that really matter. When your to do list gets overwhelming that's when you got to tap into the power of discipline.

Let me be honest with you—staying disciplined can be challenging initially, and it's tempting to give up. It's like trying to tame an animal or mastering a dance step. But here's the beautiful part: the more you practice, the easier it gets. Eventually, it becomes the foundation that keeps your success story intact.

As I shared a bit of my journey earlier, I was completely lost when I first started going to the gym. I didn't know how to use half the equipment and certainly didn't feel confident being there. But I showed up. Day after day, I walked into that gym feeling like a beginner. When you lack motivation to do what must be achieved, discipline steps in; it is the guiding force that propels you towards your objectives when distractions beckon.

Slowly, through consistency and practice, I started to see progress. That experience taught me that success in fitness, much like anything else, isn't about instant results—it's about showing up, putting in the work, and trusting the process.

Over time, the discipline I developed in the gym didn't just improve my physical health; it spilled over into other areas of my life. I found myself more focused at work, more determined to stick to my goals, and more capable of handling the challenges that came my way. Whether it was pushing through a challenging workout or tackling a difficult project at work, the lesson was the same:

> Success is built on small, consistent actions that compound over time.

This lesson became even more crucial when it came to managing my health. Like many of us, I've faced those days when I didn't feel like exercising or eating right. I wanted to take shortcuts or skip a session because it felt too hard. But I realised that discipline isn't just about doing things when it's easy; it's about doing them when it's hard, when you don't feel like it, and when everything else is tempting you to quit.

And that's what separates fleeting efforts from long-lasting results.

Practice:

Then there's practice. To become better at anything we do, we have to do it over and over again. Most people say "practice makes perfect," but I prefer to say

> Practice makes improvement.

Why? Because when we practice something a few times, we become better, not perfect. It has never been about becoming perfect—no, not at all. It's more about something yet meaningful: progress. Perfection is an impossible standard, but improvement is always within reach.

Therefore, it's through repetition that we truly begin to excel. Each time you practice, you improve a bit more. And here's the amazing part—there is always space for growth. You may never hit that 100% perfection threshold, and that's perfectly fine. The important thing is how you develop, change and strive to be the version of yourself. Your path involves challenging yourself aiming for new heights and understanding that there's always another summit to reach.

Every time you practice, whether it's honing a skill, learning something new, or even working out, you get a little bit better. And that improvement fuels your motivation to keep going.

Always do your best:

Imagine starting your day with excitement, knowing that each day presents an opportunity for growth and progress, an opportunity to be better than yesterday. It sounds pretty great, doesn't it? Well, it's not just a wish – it's entirely achievable with the right attitude and mindset.

Here's the deal: we often compare our journey to that of others. We witness someone's accomplishments and question why we haven't reached similar heights. But here's a little secret: measuring your progress against others won't lead you far. Instead, focus on comparing yourself to who you were yesterday. Let me explain further.

Picture setting a goal for yourself today. Whether embarking on writing a book, mastering a skill or enhancing your well-being, the key is to concentrate on improving and always giving your best. Let’s say you opt to pursue writing a book. The initial days may pose challenges, you might grapple with finding the words and face moments of self-doubt. However, if you commit to enhancing yourself by 1% each day something remarkable begins to unfold. By the end of 10 days, you'll already notice a 10% improvement in your endeavours.

It may not appear significant, but remember, you're not starting a new thing each day. You're building upon the progress you achieved the previous day. Now, fast forward to 90 days.

At that point, writing will feel easy to you. Tasks that used to take hours will now only require a fraction of that time. Your confidence, in your abilities will be higher. Your words will carry a clarity and purpose.

Embracing this mindset opens up possibilities. You see, it's not just about progress; it's about the impact over time. Similar to interest, small improvements accumulate gradually. It is the "compound effect." For example, you'll be astonished at how you've progressed by the end of the year. You'll see a 365% improvement from where you stand today. Can you imagine this?

<u>Persistence</u>:

Now, all of what I mentioned above alone isn’t enough. A common trait among some of the dynamic minds is their unwavering persistence. They persist until they achieve their desired outcomes. Persistence separates the dreamers from the doers. Imagine setting a goal for yourself. It's easy to talk and write about your big goals or get excited about new plans. But true success requires the determination to keep showing up, making it a daily habit to revisit your goal while taking steps towards its realisation, even when it’s tough and when you’d rather do something else.

The thing is, persistence isn't about putting in effort when it's convenient. It involves taking action every time a task arises, no matter what else is happening in your life.

Whether it may be a sports game, a coffee outing with a friend, or a tempting Netflix marathon beckoning you, the secret is to prioritise your responsibilities and stick to your routine. This is where discipline I mentioned earlier plays a role.

One of the most valuable lessons I learned from my mentoring sessions with Jack Canfield involves the concept of persistence. In his book The Success Principles, Jack presents 64 principles for achieving success, and among them is "Practice Persistence" as a cornerstone. This principle emphasises the importance of not giving up on our goals. It's about persisting and moving forward even in challenging times. This reminds me of Albert Einstein's quote,

> "Insanity is doing the same thing over and over again and expecting different results."

Take a moment to think about children. Have you ever noticed how determined they can be when they desire something? They will repeatedly ask for it, convinced that they will eventually get it. They don't worry about fear of rejection. They simply persist because deep down they understand that persistence yields results. This same relentless drive is what we need to adopt as adults, but often, we hold ourselves back. We hesitate to seek help, request a pay rise, look for investment for our businesses or step out of our comfort zones.

Instead, we frequently remain stagnant in territory, reluctant to push our boundaries.

Persistence is the key to breaking through these barriers. It's the belief that, even if success doesn't come immediately, it will come eventually as long as we keep trying. Take Thomas Edison and his creation of the bulb, for instance. They say he failed more than 1,000 times before he finally succeeded. When questioned about his failures, he famously remarked,

> I have not failed. I've discovered 1,000 ways that won't work.

Edison recognised that each attempt brought him nearer to success. He didn't see failure as a reason to give up but as an essential part of the journey. He knew deep down it would work but had no idea how, but he kept testing repeatedly. After 1000+ attempts, he found out the way for it to work. Edison's perseverance paid off in the end. Through his dedication, we now have the light bulb, a groundbreaking invention that has transformed the world. Imagine, if Edison had given up after a setback, we might still be sitting in the dark or burning candles to have a light source.

Now, don't get me wrong. I am not asking you to be persistent about something that is obviously not going to work. Persistence goes beyond pushing blindly; it involves learning and adjusting with each try. It means having such a belief in your objective that you're willing to encounter obstacles and continue moving.

It's about realising that every "no" brings you closer to a "yes."

And that's the power of having a dynamic mindset. It's like the filter that shapes how you see the world. Your mindset reflects your attitude, beliefs and approach to challenges and opportunities. Consider it like wearing glasses that can either provide clarity or cloud your vision. When you adopt a dynamic mindset, like people such as Thomas Edison and other legends who believed in improvement through effort and learning, it's as if you're putting on glasses that bring the world into focus. They viewed challenges as opportunities for growth, constantly pushing forward, even in the face of setbacks.

Meanwhile, life can get overwhelmingly busy, and the temptation to put things off until "later" becomes strong. But here's the blunt reality: if you let that mindset of procrastination creep in, "later" often morphs into "never," and the potential for growth slips away. Balancing a dynamic mindset with life's busyness is key to seizing those moments for growth instead of letting them vanish.

Instead of procrastinating, it is crucial to recognise when something enjoyable is on the horizon and consciously choose to tackle your tasks first.

Here's my approach: I remind myself, "I will complete this task before saying yes to any fun activity."

It may sound simple, but it holds power. It compels me to manage my time and make space for what matters.

Don't get me wrong; having fun is actually important to staying balanced and preventing burnout. The trick is to see it as a treat—something to enjoy after finishing your work. Picture it like this: After you finish a task, you're giving yourself a deserved break. Whether it's grabbing coffee with a friend or going out to watch a game, it's an opportunity to relax and acknowledge your achievements.

So, success becomes simple when it comes down to mastering these four elements: discipline, practice, doing your best, and persistence. They're not flashy, but they're effective. As I shared above, they helped me transform my health in the gym. In my work, they helped me stay focused and achieve more than I thought possible. And in life, they've been the driving force behind every accomplishment I've experienced.

The good news is that these principles are available to anyone willing to commit. No matter where you are in your journey—whether you're just starting out or trying to reach that next level—success is within your reach. And it's a lot simpler than it might seem, and we will explore more of that in the next chapter.

SOLVE SMARTER, NOT HARDER

As I emphasised earlier, good health encompasses not just the body but also the mind. Maintaining health involves exercising your mind just as you would exercise your body at the gym. Engaging in activities such as reading, meditation, and puzzle solving, like working on a Rubric Cube, helps create connections in your brain, leading to improved problem-solving abilities and keeping the mind sharp.

You see, challenges are a part of life. The more challenges you overcome, the more fulfilling life becomes. The more problems you solve, the better your life becomes. But you need to understand that avoiding problems doesn't make them disappear; it only makes them bigger, more complex and challenging to handle. Sometimes, we overlook issues that appear simple to resolve, leading us to procrastinate. However, these small problems can escalate quickly demanding time and mental effort for resolution. So, the key is to take action.

How You View Problems Matters

As you already know, personal development is a continuous journey that involves honing your skills, expanding your knowledge, and evolving to a more dynamic mindset. One key aspect of this journey is how you approach the inevitable problems that arise. Problems can be perceived differently, and how you view a situation can determine how easy or difficult it is to solve.

<u>Here's a quick exercise to illustrate this</u>:

Look at the picture below, which shows a row of parking spaces. The numbers are visible on the empty spaces but not on the spaces where the car is parked. Your task is to guess the number of hidden parking spaces. Please take a couple of minutes to think about it before jumping to conclusions.

This exercise demonstrates that sometimes, stepping back and viewing the problem from a different angle can make the solution much more obvious and with a dynamic mindset, tackling challenges can become more manageable and enjoyable.

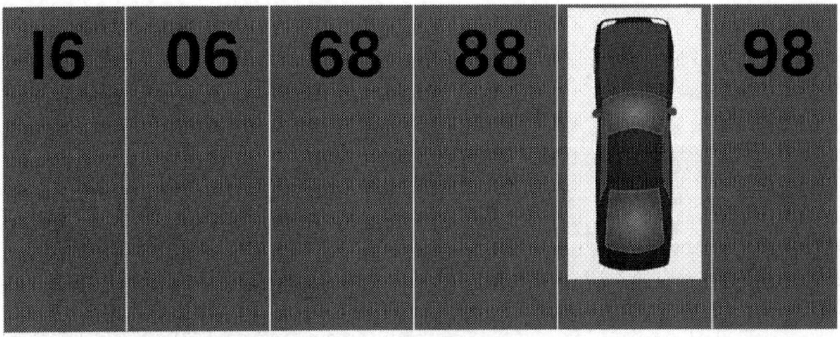

Did you manage to solve the problem? If yes, well done!

You have a truly creative mind. If not, don't worry—I'm here to show you how easy it can be. Now, here's a little twist: try turning the book upside down and see if you're able to solve the problem now.

Did that help? If yes, fantastic!

This simple exercise shows that whether a problem feels hard or easy often depends entirely on the perspective you're using to approach it. That's why I firmly believe a good mindset can make all the difference in any situation in life.

Interestingly, many people find it easier to fulfil favours for others but struggle to stay committed to their goals. Can you relate to this? Why does this discrepancy exist? Allow me to share an anecdote that sheds light on this issue. Once, while working at a client's residence, I was asked to perform a task that I was reluctant to undertake. In response to how I felt, I cited company policy as grounds for refusal. I said, "I can't do it because is against our policy". The client paused momentarily before remarking, "The company is yours, right?"

Taken aback, I affirmed this fact. The client then suggested, "If it's your company, you set the rules and the policy. You have the authority to bend them; no one will object."

After a pause for reflection, I replied with certainty, "Indeed, I established those policies; hence, I adhere to them. I crafted this policy to outline how our business should function. If I violate it, it may benefit you. It won't serve the interests of my business. Therefore, I regret to say. The answer is no."

At that moment, I followed my instincts impulsively. You know what?

Since then, I've adhered to the policy wholeheartedly. Sure, I've made some modifications along the way, but always for the better. As you can see, it is all about how we perceive a problem.
As Bob Proctor wisely said,

> Success is 5% strategy and 95% mindset.

And I couldn't agree more. There are so many ways to think about a problem, but this perspective is one of the most powerful for understanding the importance of mindset. As I mentioned earlier, a person with a poor mindset might say, "I can't do this," while someone with a dynamic mindset will ask, "How can I do this?" It's no coincidence that some people go on to build wealth and success while others struggle.

Having a dynamic mindset is the key difference.

Think about it: why do you think so many people who win the lottery end up broke again within three years? And why, if a successful person loses everything, can they often rebuild their fortune, sometimes even greater than before?

It all comes down to mindset. It's living proof that cultivating a dynamic mindset isn't just about getting rich in terms of money but also about becoming wealthy in every area of life—whether that's relationships, personal growth, or happiness.

Remember that tackling life's challenges doesn't have to be overwhelming or take a toll on you mentally and physically. In fact, a few simple strategies can make all the difference. We all face problems—big and small—whether at work, in relationships, or just in the everyday hustle. How we handle them determines not only the outcome but also how much stress they bring into our lives.

As we are getting close to the end of this chapter, here are some practical steps you can take to deal with problems effectively without letting them drain your energy:

1. Address Issues Promptly: We've all been there—putting off that uncomfortable conversation, ignoring that nagging task, or waiting until the last minute to deal with a challenge. But here's the truth is that the longer you wait, the bigger the problem becomes. Addressing issues as soon as they arise prevents them from snowballing into something more stressful. It's like ripping off a Band-Aid—short-term discomfort for long-term relief. Whether it's a challenging work task or a personal conflict, dealing with it early can save you a ton of headaches (and heartaches) later.

2. Break Down Issues: Big problems can feel paralysing, and it's easy to get overwhelmed when facing something insurmountable. The key is to break the issue down into smaller, manageable tasks. Instead of thinking, "I need to solve this entire problem right now," focus on one small step you can take today.

This approach makes even the most challenging situations feel more doable, and each small win builds momentum. You'll chip away at the problem bit by bit without feeling like you're drowning in it.

3. Maintain Consistency: Consistency is the secret sauce to avoiding chaos. When you work on resolving issues regularly —whether it's daily or weekly—you prevent things from piling up. It's like maintaining a clean house; if you tidy up a little each day, it never gets overwhelming. The same goes for your challenges. Keep taking small, consistent actions to tackle problems; you'll be amazed at how much lighter life feels.

It's all about proactive action. The more you practice these strategies, the less likely you are to feel crushed under the weight of problems. You'll find yourself handling challenges more efficiently and keeping your mental and physical well-being intact. Remember, it's not about being perfect or solving everything at once—it's about making steady progress and not letting problems take control of your life.

So, next time something comes up, take a deep breath, break it down, and tackle it head-on. You've got this!

Okay, as we wrap up this chapter, here is a small reminder again that life often feels like a whirlwind—trying to juggle work, family, social commitments, and personal goals all at once. It can feel like a constant balancing act, with your attention pulled in a thousand directions.

We tell ourselves that everything will fall into place if we work a little harder, make a little more money, or reach that next milestone. But as we have explored together in this chapter, the real foundation for everything else—success, happiness, even wealth—is your health.

It is a principle that many overlook until it's too late. It's easy to chase after the external markers of success—the big house, the fancy car, the hefty bank account—but what's the point of all that if you're running on empty? If you're too stressed, exhausted, or unwell to enjoy it? Take time to reflect on what really matters to you. Is it being present with the people you love? Pursuing your passions with enthusiasm? Feeling vibrant and full of life each day? As Jessen James would say,

> "Elevate your awareness"

Become aware of the things that make life meaningful, yet we often push them aside in the rush to "succeed." But when you start prioritising your health, everything changes. True wealth is about being mentally sharp, emotionally stable, and physically strong enough to handle whatever life throws your way.

Without well-being, all the money in the world won't bring you joy, energy, or peace.

So, what's your next step?

This shift isn't about making drastic changes overnight. It's about one intentional step at a time. Embracing a dynamic mindset means being open to change and recognising that progress comes from small, consistent actions. Take action today—whether it's going for a walk, cooking a healthy meal, or simply taking a moment to breathe deeply.

Prioritise yourself, and watch as every other aspect of your life flourishes. Remember, you can't pour from an empty cup. If you constantly put yourself last, everything else will eventually suffer. Adopting a dynamic mindset encourages you to view these moments of self-care not as luxuries but as necessities. So, start today. Commit to prioritising yourself—not just for your own sake but for the people who count on you.

When you care for your well-being, you're laying the foundation for a more prosperous, more fulfilled life, where success isn't just about what you've accumulated but how you feel every day. This mindset shift opens up new possibilities and allows you to approach challenges with resilience and clarity.

So, fill yours first, and everything else will follow.

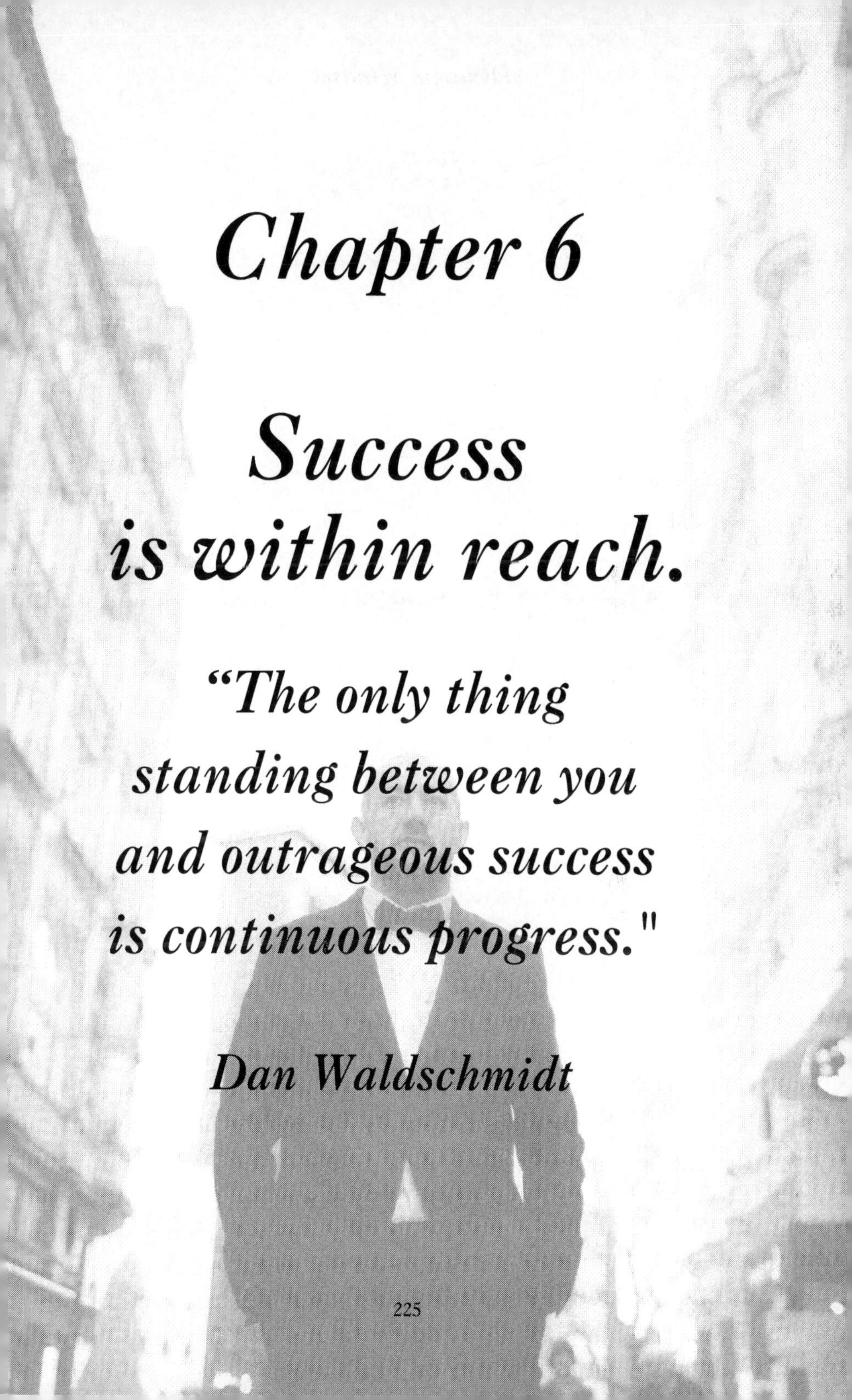

Chapter 6

Success is within reach.

"The only thing standing between you and outrageous success is continuous progress."

Dan Waldschmidt

SUCCESS IS WITHIN REACH

As we reach the end of our journey through a Dynamic Mindset, it's important to take a moment to reflect on how far we've come. You've embarked on a path that's not just about change but about growth and continuous evolution. The concept of success, which might have once felt distant or elusive, is now within your grasp.

In the previous chapters, we've explored the importance of resilience, navigated the challenges of responsibility, embraced the uncertainty of new beginnings, unlocked the tools for growth, and recognized the profound connection between wellness and wealth. This final chapter is dedicated to tying together all the concepts we've explored, leaving you with a clear roadmap to apply these insights in your life.

SUCCESS IS CLOSER THAN YOU THINK

From the outset, we've explored that success isn't as distant as it sometimes feels. Success, in its truest sense, is already within your grasp. The dynamic mindset is your key to unlocking it. You've learned to see challenges not as roadblocks but as opportunities to grow, adapt, and persevere.

Success is within reach

Remember the story of the gold miner from Napoleon Hill's Think and Grow Rich? One of its standout teachings revolves around the concept of being "3 feet from gold". This analogy originates from the era of the gold rush of a young man who dedicated months to mining for gold. Fuelled by optimism and unwavering dedication, he tirelessly kept digging but found no trace of gold. Exhausted and demoralised, he eventually gave up and decided to sell his tools to a "junk man" for a fraction of their value. However, this junk man was unlike any other; prior to delving into mining himself, he sought counsel from an expert. The expert surveyed the mine. He was determined that the gold lay three feet beyond where the young man had stopped digging. With resolve and expert guidance, the junk man resumed digging and struck gold.

These principles remind us that success isn't the product of luck or external factors but a result of inner transformation and persistence—a concept that aligns with everything we've explored in Dynamic Mindset. As we've observed, this mindset drives determination, which is frequently the defining factor between those who achieve their goals and those who don't. You can attain the desired success by immersing yourself in learning and putting what you have learned into practice with commitment and perseverance.

Success is often closer than you think, and your path to achieving it is unique. I will give you the fundamental elements to help you create your success blueprint.

The truth is that we often give up just before our breakthrough. Remember that when the road gets tough, you might be only one step away from your "gold."

CRAFT YOUR SUCCESS BLUEPRINT

Now, let's pull it all together. Success isn't just about following a path someone else has laid out for you. It's about designing your own. As we explore how to craft your success blueprint, keep in mind that you can't pursue someone else's idea of success, just like you wouldn't wear someone else's shoes and expect them to fit perfectly. Your blueprint is yours alone, guiding you toward the life you want to build.

In no particular order, here are the foundations you should contemplate as you create your success blueprint:

Define Your Values

Take some time to reflect on what's most important to you. Whether it's family, creativity, financial freedom, or health, make sure your actions align with your values.

Each of us holds values that shape our beliefs and choices. Values are important to us and guide our decisions. At times, however, we may compromise these values to meet others' expectations, leading us away from our true path.
For instance, imagine I value growth and decide to set aside time from 8 PM to 10 PM to work on my book.

Then, a friend invites me to hang out, and I go out, fearing I might disappoint them. This is where things become complex. Prioritising my friend's request over my goals means aligning with their agenda, not mine.

This happens all the time. But here's the key: you always have a choice. You can say no. In my case, the decision is 100% my responsibility because I had access to my phone, saw the message and chose to respond. Now, a tactic I've found effective in handling situations like this is establishing boundaries with my phone. As I shared in the previous chapter, I habitually keep my phone on silent mode in another room while focusing on important tasks. Since adopting this practice, I've noticed a boost in my productivity.

I get more done in less time, which means I manage my time efficiently, allowing me time to complete tasks and, most importantly, quality moments with myself, my family and my friends.

Your values guide your choices, and by setting boundaries, you've learned will protect what matters most.

Challenge Your Mindset

Let's break that down into two key elements: your way of thinking and your opinions.

Way of Thinking: The way you think isn't just shaped by random thoughts—it's influenced by the mental programs already installed in your mind from past experiences. Every one of us interprets the world differently based on these programs. For example, think about how we once viewed technology. If someone in the early 1900s saw a person talking to a plastic rectangle (a smartphone), they might have thought they were insane. But today? It's completely normal.

This shift in thinking shows how our understanding and acceptance of new ideas can change dramatically over time, and it also points to a more profound truth: our beliefs shape our reality. We rely on our existing knowledge to shape our perception of the world, and since everyone's experiences are unique, no two people see the world in the same way. Our view of the world is continually evolving based on our past experiences and sensory inputs.

Your mindset can either limit or liberate you. Some people say, "Making money is hard," while others say, "Making money is easy." As discussed in the introduction, the difference isn't just their financial situation—it's their mindset. If you want to change anything in your life, you must first change how you think about that subject.

Opinions and Beliefs: Have you ever noticed that sometimes you believe in something, but deep down, you're not fully convinced? That's because belief isn't the same as knowing.

For example, you might believe in the existence of God, but you don't know God the same way you know your mother, whose presence and existence you never doubt. You're 100% certain when you know something, and that certainty fuels action. This is why transforming to a dynamic mindset is key. When you shift from believing you might achieve something to knowing you will, that's when real change happens.

To create your blueprint for success, you must first lay the foundation—a dynamic mindset. This means constantly challenging your beliefs, shifting your thinking, and staying open to new possibilities. A flexible, evolving mindset is vital to unlocking the growth and success you're aiming for.

Set Boundaries

Setting boundaries is crucial to maintaining alignment with your blueprint for success. In today's tech-driven world, distractions are everywhere, and social media is a major culprit. Many people unknowingly fall into the trap of social media, spending hours consuming content instead of focusing on what truly matters to them. I've experienced this firsthand. In the past, I spent a significant amount of my "free time" scrolling through social platforms. After reflecting on the hours I wasted, I realised I could have used that time more productively—perhaps starting a side business or dedicating time to personal growth through reading.

This is where boundaries come into play. Social media, while enjoyable, often leaves us feeling unfulfilled when we're simply consuming content rather than creating or growing. It's easy to blame lack of time or finances for not pursuing our goals, but the truth is, we all have the time—we need to take control over how we use it.

One of my best practices is to silence my phone and leave it in another room while working on important tasks. This small step has had a significant impact on my productivity. Without constant interruptions, I can focus deeply on my priorities and, as a result, accomplish far more. By prioritising your tasks and saying no to distractions, you not only become more efficient but also align your actions with your values.

As mentioned in Chapter 5, a dynamic mindset thrives on focus and discipline. Setting boundaries with your time, energy, and technology allows you to stay committed to your goals. When you document your goals, review them regularly, and work toward them consistently, you're building a mindset that can overcome obstacles and achieve remarkable success.

In the end, it's about taking control of how you spend your time and ensuring that your efforts are channelled toward the things that truly matter to you. That's the power of a dynamic mindset—staying focused on your aspirations, no matter the distractions around you.

Stay Consistent

Success doesn't happen overnight. It's built day by day, decision by decision. As we touched base about this in Chapter 5, Consistency plays a massive role in achieving success, and if there's one thing I've learned from going to the gym, it's just how powerful that consistency can be. Like Jessen James always says,

> "Consistency is what pays off."

The more you stick with something, the more natural it becomes; over time, it becomes easier to maintain. When I started going to the gym, it instilled discipline in me, not just in fitness but in various aspects of life. When you set a goal and work towards it consistently, you start to see progress, even if it's slow at first.

And that progress? It's like fuel for your motivation. Once you notice that you're moving forward, even just a little, that progress will fuel your determination to persevere.

Now, maybe the gym isn't your thing—and that's totally fine! You could be learning a new skill, working towards a personal or professional goal, or just trying to improve at something you care about. The key is putting in the regular effort, day in and day out because real, lasting results don't come from bursts of intense effort—they come from steady, consistent progress over time.

Every little step you take counts, even if it feels small or insignificant at the moment.

Eventually, those small steps add up, and before you know it, you're closer to your goal than you ever thought you'd be. It's important to remember that no matter how big or intimidating the task might seem, the key is to keep at it.
I learned that going to the gym once in a while won't make a difference. Even if you go every day for a month, you might not see the results you're hoping for.

It wasn't until I committed to a routine—going at least three times a week for several months—that I started to see real improvements. That's when the change began to happen. It wasn't about doing something drastic but showing up, putting in the effort consistently, and trusting that the results would follow.

When I first started going to the gym, I had absolutely no clue how to use any equipment. It was pretty intimidating, to be honest. I'd look around at everyone who seemed to know exactly what they were doing and feel completely lost. But with regular visits, some trial and error, and observing others, I slowly started getting the hang of it. Every gym session became less about "just working out" and more of an opportunity for learning and personal development.

The cool thing is, while this example is about the gym, the principle applies to just about everything in life.

Whether it's your career, a hobby, or any personal goal, you've got to stay open to learning—and sometimes even relearning things you might've forgotten.

Growth happens when you allow yourself to be a beginner and remain curious. But here's the thing: I know it's easy to say that and much more challenging to stick with it. If you've ever struggled to stay consistent with something—whether it's an exercise routine, a new skill, or any other objective—believe me, I get it. Life throws off days at you, and that's completely normal. What really matters is not letting those off days turn into an off week or an off month.

The key is getting back on track as soon as you can.

Now, let's be honest. We all have distractions, right? Take Netflix, for example. Many people spend hours binge-watching shows on it, and hey, there's nothing wrong with that if it aligns with their goals. But for me, I make sure that when I do watch something, it contributes to my growth in some way. So, instead of mindlessly watching TV, I'll choose mindset videos, motivational content, or documentaries that teach me something new. It's about being intentional with how you spend your time, even when you're relaxing.

I usually set aside around an hour each day to watch empowering videos—not once, but spread out throughout the day. I believe that watching affirmation and motivational videos can be impactful, especially when I'm feeling off course.

Taking a break to watch one video for five minutes helps me refocus and come back to my tasks with renewed strength, motivation and positivity. Now, one crucial thing to bear in mind is, as I mentioned earlier, finding a balance between learning and taking action is essential. While watching content and expanding your knowledge is beneficial, applying what you've learned is equally important. Action is the key that transforms knowledge into outcomes. So don't just absorb information – put it into practice.

Train your mind

For me, it all began with a 3x3 Rubik's Cube. Years ago, I became fascinated by its complexity but never quite managed to solve it. Then, around five years back, my son showed me how to solve it, and that changed everything. Since then, solving the Rubik's Cube has become a part of my routine. Every day, I find myself picking it up and solving it five times in each session, doing this consistently for about six days a week.

But here's the thing—it's not about speed or showcasing my skills. Solving the Rubik's Cube is a way for me to clear my mind. When I start working on it, all my stressful or distracting thoughts fade away. By the time I'm on my third solve, my brain is already focusing on positive and productive thinking. I'm not suggesting that you hurry out to buy a Rubik's Cube and start practising. What works for me may not work for you.

The main point here is finding something that helps shift your focus. For me, it happens to be the Rubik's Cube; for you, it could be something else. The only way to find out is to start exploring different brain teasers.

In addition to solving the Rubik's Cube, I find joy in playing brain games such as Sudoku and crossword puzzles. These activities serve a purpose. They stimulate parts of my mind and enhance my thinking abilities. They are like exercises that keep my mind alert and adaptable.

Consider your brain as a muscle. Just like we don't expect results from working out at the gym, we shouldn't expect changes in our mental prowess. Similar to targeting muscle groups during workouts (like biceps, triceps, chest, and legs), our brain benefits from challenges focusing on problem-solving, memory retention, and learning skills. Similar to how a rounded workout regimen strengthens our body, engaging in mental tasks helps keep our brains sharp. Regularly pushing our limits can enhance cognitive functions, foster creativity and promote general well-being.

So, take a moment and think: What's your preferred way to exercise your mind? It could involve any activity that stimulates your brain and encourages thinking outside the box, whether it's reading books, playing chess, learning a language, or diving into pursuits like painting or writing. The key is finding something that encourages you to approach problems from different perspectives.

Perseverance

As discussed in Chapter 5, perseverance is essential to mastering change that will take you steps closer to success, whether in your daily habits or long-term goals. Just as we form habits that guide our daily routines, we can reshape them, unlocking new opportunities for growth.

Consider something as simple as getting dressed. After repeating the routine for a while, it becomes natural. Maybe you always put on your right shoe first, without even thinking about it, right? That's because your mind has made it a habit, probably all the way back when your parents helped you put your shoes on. But if you pay attention, you can change that habit. Try putting on your left shoe first instead of your usual right. At first, it might feel strange or awkward, but that's only because you're so used to your current habit. The interesting thing about habits is that they feel natural simply because we've repeated them so many times. However, with a bit of persistence, you have the power to change them. What feels unfamiliar now can eventually become second nature.

Take a similar example with your hands: if you naturally cross your fingers, place one pinkie on the bottom, which feels comfortable. Now, if you uncross your fingers and shift them so the other pinkie ends up on the bottom, it will likely feel uncomfortable or awkward. But, just like switching the order of your shoes, the discomfort fades with time.

With consistency, even that unfamiliar sensation will become your new routine, just like putting on your left shoe first.

In the end, persistence is the driving force that keeps you moving toward success. Collaborate with your subconscious, trust the process, and remain committed to your goals. What feels uncomfortable or unfamiliar now will soon become second nature; before you know it, the change you seek will be a part of who you are. Your breakthrough is closer than you think.

Embrace the power of Affirmations

Affirmations are like seeds planted in the garden of your mind. They are declarations of your intentions and desires, spoken as if they are already a reality. When nurtured, affirmations have the power to shape your beliefs, attitudes, and actions, guiding you toward the life you want to create. Take Cristiano Ronaldo, for example—arguably one of the greatest footballers ever. Before every free kick, he motivates himself with affirmations like, "I am the best," "I'm going to score," and "I will win." His confidence is a big part of what drives his record-breaking success, showing just how powerful affirmations can be when truly believed.

That said, when you start using affirmations, they might feel strange or ineffective. Feeling some resistance is normal—your subconscious might push back against these new ideas. However, like any habit, affirmations need practice and consistency to work.

At first, it might feel like you're just repeating empty words. But over time, with persistence, something remarkable happens.

As you continue repeating your affirmations, you'll start to notice changes in your mindset and actions. The doubts and fears that once held you back will start to fade. You'll find yourself becoming more confident, capable, and aligned with your goals. It's just like planting a seed: at first, there's nothing visible above the surface, but beneath, roots are growing—eventually, the seed sprouts and blossoms into something beautiful.

In much the same way, affirmations may seem small and insignificant at first, but they can significantly transform your life over time. As Napoleon Hill famously said,

> “Whatever the mind can conceive and believe, it can achieve.”

So don't get discouraged if you don't see immediate results from your affirmations. Keep planting those seeds of intention, nurture them with faith and patience, and soon enough, you'll see the fruits of your efforts. Whether you need a lot of nurturing or just a little, the key is to keep at it.

Personally, I used to carry a card in my wallet with my affirmations, reading them every morning and evening. Now, I've taken a photo of it and made it my phone's lock screen.

I see it every time I unlock my phone—often over 50 times a day. Even though I know them by heart, having them constantly in front of me keeps me focused and reminded of what I'm working toward.

Affirmations, like seeds, will eventually grow and bear fruit as long as you continue to believe in and nurture them. With persistence and faith, you'll align your life with your dreams.

Understand how the Law of Attraction works

Creating the life you want might seem daunting, but it becomes easier if you understand the process. You have probably heard about the law of attraction, and it seems easy, but think about it: it's not that simple. Most people don't understand it, and I have been one of them for years. The law of attraction dictates that like attracts like, meaning your thoughts and emotions attract similar experiences and outcomes. However, it's not just about thinking positively and waiting for things to happen.

Taking action is Key.

For example, let's say you want a new pair of shoes. According to the law of attraction, you would visualise yourself wearing the shoes and feel the joy they bring you. But for this to truly work, you also need to take action, like going out and buying them. It's a combination of mindset and action that brings the results.

Now, let me share a different perspective with you. Have you ever thought about how certain words carry more meanings than we initially perceive? Let's consider the word "attraction." When broken down it becomes three words, "at tr action." If you look up the meaning of "TR," you'll discover that it stands for "translation." Therefore, attraction can be viewed as ", at translation action." What does this suggest?

Simply put, it indicates that attraction is inherently linked to taking action. It's not about hoping or asking the universe to fulfil your wishes; it's actively moving towards them.

Engaging in meditation can help you visualise your aspirations endlessly. Without action, those aspirations will merely remain fantasies. Meditation proves beneficial as it heightens your awareness of your surroundings and enhances creativity. This increased awareness and creativity play a role in identifying opportunities and initiating action. It's similar to being provided with a map and a compass; however, you must take those steps to reach your desired destination.

Practice Gratitude

In today's fast-paced world, it's easy to lose sight of the abundance that already surrounds us. But by cultivating a habit of gratitude—acknowledging and appreciating what we already have—we can shift our focus to the positive aspects of our lives.

Gratitude isn't just about material things; it also encompasses the emotions and feelings that bring richness to our lives. Recognising their value can bring a sense of contentment and peace, whether it's something as simple as a comfortable pair of shoes or as significant as a home or business. But gratitude goes beyond what we feel for ourselves. It's also about acknowledging how others see us. Too often, we dismiss the importance of expressing gratitude for the compliments or kind words we receive from others. When someone praises you, instead of brushing it off, pause and genuinely say "thank you."

Accepting praise with sincere gratitude not only nurtures your sense of self-worth but also honours the person giving the compliment.

It's common to feel awkward or undeserving when receiving compliments; some might downplay the praise to avoid discomfort. However, in doing so, we miss out on the positive energy and connection that gratitude can foster. By gracefully accepting kind words, we strengthen our relationships and uplift our spirits.

Incorporating gratitude into our daily lives doesn't just change how we see the world—it transforms our relationships and brings a deep sense of fulfilment. So, I encourage you to make gratitude a guiding principle in your life. Embrace it fully, and see how it enriches your perspective, strengthens your connections, and brings more joy into your everyday experiences.

Whatever it is, know that you're equipped with the mindset, tools, and resilience to make it happen. Your success is closer than you think—so keep digging, keep believing, and keep striving. The gold may be within reach.

Don't give up before reaching your wealth—I know I won't! I want you to know that I am grateful for you and the energy you bring to this journey. Your commitment to embracing a dynamic mindset is inspiring and a testament to the incredible potential within each of you. Remember, whatever challenges you face, you are equipped with the mindset, tools, and resilience to make your dreams a reality. Your success is closer than you think—so keep digging, keep believing, and keep striving.

The gold may be within reach, and I firmly believe that you have the power to achieve it.

Don't give up before reaching your wealth—I know I won't!

With Gratitude and Confidence in you

Gracias

Manuel Gonçalves

"Never give up, for that is just the place and time that the tide will turn."

—Harriet Beecher Stowe

Printed in Great Britain
by Amazon

49673055R00137